Our God Still Speaks

OUR GOD
STILL SPEAKS

REAL-LIFE STORIES OF HOW GOD ANSWER PRAYERS - BOOK 1

VIRGINIA STEWART METZLER

ReadersMagnet, LLC

Our God Still Speaks: Real-life Stories Of How God Answer Prayers – Book 1
Copyright © 2023 by Virginia Stewart Metzler

Published in the United States of America

Library of Congress Control Number: 2024917452
ISBN   Paperback: 979-8-89091-705-8
ISBN   eBook: 979-8-89091-706-5

All rights reserved. No part of this publication may be reproduced, stored in a retrieval system or transmitted in any way by any means, electronic, mechanical, photocopy, recording or otherwise without the prior permission of the author except as provided by USA copyright law.

The opinions expressed by the author are not necessarily those of ReadersMagnet, LLC.

ReadersMagnet, LLC
10620 Treena Street, Suite 230 | San Diego, California, 92131 USA
1.619. 354. 2643 | www.readersmagnet.com

Book design copyright © 2023 by ReadersMagnet, LLC. All rights reserved.

Cover design by Tifanny Curaza
Interior design by Dorothy Lee

Table Of Contents

Introduction 7
Book Dedication 9
Acknowledgments 11

Part 1—Introduction To Life In Africa 13
Chapter 1: Unexpected Gifts 16
Chapter 2: The Dumpling 23
Chapter 3: Rain, Corks And Snakes 27
Chapter 4: Terror In The Sky 30
Chapter 5: When Not To Shoot A Crocodile 37
Chapter 6: The Day Of The Driver Ant Invasion 42
Chapter 7: Living Out Ecclesiastes Chapter 3 46

Part 2—Life Back In The States 66
Chapter 8: Falling Head Over Heels 68
Chapter 9: The Road To Ethiopia 77
Chapter 10: Taking Spanish And Other Lessons 88
Chapter 11: When God Changes Your Plans 94

Part 3—Introduction To Life In Ilap 100
Chapter 12: The Borrowed Blanket 105
Chapter 13: The Butterfly Tree 105
Chapter 14: Searching For A Quiet Place 117
Chapter 15: Green Beans And Other Miracles 120
Chapter 16: More Than Rice 127

Chapter 17: Never Trust A Rock In The River..................................... 132
Chapter 18: What Fellowship Has Light With Darkness?...................... 136
Chapter 19: Dinner With Donny And Marie... 142
Chapter 20: Helping The Blind To See... 145
Chapter 21: The Bog... 153
Chapter 22: Look Who's Watching.. 158
Chapter 23: Under The Circumstances.. 161
Chapter 24: The Two Brothers 166
Chapter 25: Three Words You Never Want To Hear 159
Chapter 26: Visiting Sparrows... 173

Part 4—Life After Ilap 177
Chapter 27: The Best Sore Throat I Ever Had 179
Chapter 28: The Best Sermon I Ever Saw 181
Chapter 29: The Adoption 184

The Epilogue 203

Introduction

The fact that God still speaks today is undeniable. This book is proof of that. In addition, we have a long, well-documented, written legacy of God's speaking to men and women throughout both the Old Testament and New Testament Scriptures.

Our God Still Speaks was written because I wanted you to read actual accounts of God speaking clearly to Les and me.

And if He spoke clearly to us, two ordinary servants, He can and will speak clearly to you.

As you read this book, my desire is that you will begin to see and experience God speaking to YOU in your own hearts and lives as well.

Book Dedication

This book is dedicated to:

Those who doubt God's personal involvement in their lives; Those who doubt God's faithfulness; Those who desire to move closer to God; Those who doubt that God still answers prayer;

Those who doubt that God still speaks to us today; and especially to

My Heavenly Father, His Son, and the Holy Spirit

who have left their handprints

all over my life and my heart as well.

Psalm 115:1

"Not to us, O Lord, not to us but to Your name be the glory, because of Your love and faithfulness."

Acknowledgments

There are many people whom I want to thank for their prayers, help and encouragement in writing this book. First and foremost is my husband Les, who thinks that I can do anything. Second is our adopted daughter, Hannah-Joy, who has bailed me out of many computer crises.

I also want to thank those of you who became the "galvanizing force" God used to get me to write this book: Leslie and Gordon Christian, Sondra Healy, Myrna and Paul Blancett, Pat and Allan Harris, Dave Ohlson (my "boss" in the Philippines), Peggy Dogris, Betty Powell Hiel, Rita Morgan, Mary Cocanougher, Gerrie Schaefer, Carole Sumerlin, Vicki Kennedy and Meadow Green. Elaine Atkinson, thanks for your advice and help. Pam Coons, my neighbor who helped me with my new computer problems and Carlen Cagle, whom God used to install my new computer. He also helped me to learn how to access new information that kept me typing. A special "thank you" goes to Gordon Wurster, my editorial assistant, who assisted me in proof-reading and reworking the manuscript. And I want to thank Karen, Gordon's wife, who was always there to encourage me and "lend an ear." I am indebted to all of you for demonstrating to me:

Hebrews 10:24

"Let us consider how we may spur one another on toward love and good deeds."

PART 1—INTRODUCTION TO LIFE IN AFRICA

The following true stories are little vignettes of things, people and situations that took place in the lives of my husband, John Thomas (Tommy) Barnett, Jr., and me ("Ginger"). After Tommy and I were married, we moved to Longview, Texas, the headquarters for R. G. LeTourneau's mission called "Tournata" (TURN ah tah). Some missionary orientation and training were required before our departure for Liberia, West Africa. Tommy had accepted a two-year commitment as the only pilot for LeTourneau's mission. We had been married only nine weeks when we arrived there in June 1957. Tommy was 22 years old and I was 17 and a half.

Ginger and Tommy, 1957

Tournata was located on Baffu (BAA fu) Bay, about an hour's flight from Monrovia, the capital city. Liberian National Airlines, the national airline, had only a few airstrips suitable to land their DC-3s. But most of the overseas flights landed at Robert's Field. It was an hour's drive *by car* from Monrovia to Robert's Field.

It was used by the American military during WW II It had to be kept in good repair because of all the international flights that landed there.

There were seven families and two single ladies who lived at LeTourneau's mission. One of the single ladies was a nurse and the other, an older lady, was a schoolteacher. She taught only the missionaries' children. An African man was hired to teach the African men.

The mission's primary purpose was two-fold:

1. *Allow the men to attend school to learn reading, writing and simple math; and*
2. *Teach those same men a skill to help them provide for their families.*

Since the jungle was thick with trees surrounding the mission, LeTourneau had constructed a sawmill. There the African men learned skills that helped them earn money to provide for their families. The men attended school one day and worked in the sawmill the next day. In retrospect, Tournata was very much like an advanced Peace Corps in teaching/training men who otherwise would not have had that opportunity. It was a very successful venture for the men.

Tournata had a generator that ran on fuel oil. Clyde Chappell was in charge of keeping the generator in good working condition. His skills allowed us to enjoy electricity from 5:00 AM until 10:30 PM every day. It was a workable situation for all of us.

Ray Morgret was our radio man. He scheduled ham radio communications with LeTourneau's base in Longview, Texas and with some others in Monrovia. When Tommy was flying to Monrovia, Ray would alert a contact there that he was on his way. When it was time for Tommy's return, Ray was notified that he was en route back to Tournata. And on occasion, when the airwaves were available, we could talk to our families and friends back in the States. That was a quantum leap for us in the late '50s.

There was a little church located about a quarter of a mile from Tournata. The manager for our mission was Walt Knowles, who was also our pastor there. The church was also used as the schoolhouse for the African men.

We also had a commissary that sold mainly canned goods (including Coca-Cola), laundry supplies and other non- perishable items. There was a dispensary or clinic that Tournata's nurse Frankie Howze supervised. She administered aspirin and antibiotics when needed and often delivered African babies. Frequently, she would remove splinters or stitch a wound for the sawmill workers.

In the beginning of our missionary service in Africa, Tommy and I were young and inexperienced in our walk with God. But in spite of our inexperience, God used a number of different situations, many of them common to all of us, to bring us closer to Him. As you read these stories, my prayer is that you too will sense God drawing you closer to Himself.

CHAPTER 1
Unexpected Gifts

Stepping off the plane that first morning in Africa is a moment that I will never forget. I recognized the smoky, damp and woodsy smells. But the air was also filled with pungent odors and aromas of things not familiar to me. As a young child and throughout my teen years, I had read everything at my disposal about that colorful and mysterious dark continent. Now my small, limited world exploded as I experienced for the first time the very countries and places that I had only read about. I was so awed and captivated to actually be living in Africa! Tommy and I would be living there because of Tommy's job as a pilot for LeTourneau's mission.

R. G. LeTourneau was an inventor from Longview, Texas. He invented large earth- moving equipment such as tree crushers and "stingers" (tree removers). Liberia was filled with trees in the bush, usable for lumber. Mr. LeTourneau was involved in a road building project farther down the coast near Cape Palmas. Lumber was needed for building forms for the road project. It seemed only logical to build a sawmill at Tournata. By doing that, the African men were trained to work in the sawmill. It became a useful teaching tool for them. It was not uncommon for grown African men to be illiterate. Learning to read, write and do simple arithmetic became a part of the daily schedules for those African men who worked at Tournata. I learned quickly that not every country had the advantages of an educational system available for their people.

Tournata was located on the beautiful lacy coastline between Monrovia and Cape Palmas. The coastline was a sight to behold as we flew over it! Gorgeous scalloped beaches could be seen from the air. Swaying fronds of thousands of coconut and palm- nut trees made the scene enchanting. Thatched-roof huts huddled together gave the visual appearance of a travel documentary. Behind the beaches and coconut palms grew the almost impenetrable jungle. But no one who lived there ever called, it a jungle; it was simply called "the bush."

There were so many things to learn about the country and people of Liberia. The pungent aromas (not always pleasant), beautiful views and vistas were, for the most part, delightful to my senses. There was the cacophony of sounds and languages, in addition to various nationalities of people who seemed to come from all over the world. They mesmerized me. What was there NOT to like about being in a place with all of its mysteries, colorful people, varied languages and nationalities?

Arriving in the capital city of Monrovia, there were things Tommy needed to accomplish. Some had to do with the official paperwork required for living in another country. It was necessary for him to meet people with whom he would be interfacing on his trips into Monrovia. Most of them were businessmen, selling parts and equipment that our mission needed from time to time. But then there were contacts with people rendering other services that Tournata needed. Those contacts could help point Tommy to places and people he would need to know. One African man in Monrovia, who seemed to know a lot about many things, was known only by the name "Connection." We laughed about his title, but he proved to be true to his name. When in doubt about where to find something or someone, we only had to ask Connection.

Monrovia was filled with wide streets, boulevards and concrete block buildings painted in lively colors. The "flame trees" planted along the esplanades and down the wide boulevards appeared to be set afire as the sun shone down on them. It was an enchanting scene with all the colorful people mixed together with the assortment of sights and sounds in that place called Africa.

I remember our first drive through Monrovia with the smoky smells of wood burning over the open fires. There was smoke filled, low hanging clouds in the early morning mists.

The women cooked their meals outside their huts. Still others were carrying stacks of wood balanced atop their heads. The city was filled with people who had brought produce (yams, cassava and bananas) to sell in the city. It became apparent to me that many of them were like us and were new to Monrovia. Apparently, they too had business in the city and had traveled from their homes in the countryside. It also became apparent to me that they were unfamiliar with the dangers of traffic. I was told that often they would walk into the paths of vehicles, especially the cars and large trucks, not realizing the dangers of being hurt or killed!

It was delightful for me to hear the people's voices with their various dialects. Many of them spoke in 'sing-song' melodic tones as they laughed and talked with each other.

They seemed to be such happy people as they worked side by-side. What impressed me so was that they took the time for conversation and laughter with their friends as they worked. I began to realize that my life in Liberia would be a continual learning experience. I noticed that their tasks took a backseat to their relationships with their family and friends. That realization inspired me and I planned to apply that lesson in my own life.

Before leaving Monrovia we drove to Bush Rod Island. The island was connected to the city of Monrovia by a very short bridge. There we met with Mr. Abdullah J. Abijoudi (ab ee JAO dee). Mr. Abijoudi served LeTourneau (and Tommy especially) as the "information highway." Abijoudi, as he was commonly called, was a Lebanese businessman from Beirut. Because he had lived in Liberia for quite some time, he knew a lot about everything in Monrovia. Tommy learned many things from Abijoudi: places to shop, doctors, safe places to eat, and places to find particular items our mission needed.

A special contact person in a new country was an invaluable asset for anyone, especially those of us who didn't live in Monrovia itself. Abijoudi was a charming man. His Middle Eastern, swarthy good looks and his thick accent revealed his Lebanese heritage. Our first meeting with Abijoudi was on a day when the humidity was high and the heat stifling. He kindly offered Tommy and me our very first Coca-Cola since our arrival in Africa. I had to smile about that as I drank my icy cold drink. To have Coca-Cola available to us was an unexpected gift from God. I knew then that I could live in Africa indefinitely, and particularly in Liberia. It was a small, but most-welcomed comfort to my heart.

Unlike many businessmen, Mr. Abijoudi's wife and family lived with him in Monrovia. That wasn't always the case for the businessmen who lived and worked in Liberia. Most of their wives were not willing to leave their home countries to live in AFRICA. I found that difficult to understand because I loved that beautiful continent and, in particular, that country. It was unthinkable for me to leave my husband voluntarily and to live alone in my home country!

Time limitations, both in the air and on the ground, made shopping in Monrovia a marathon for Tommy. All shopping must be done as quickly as possible so Tommy could return to Tournata before dark. Tournata had no landing lights for after- dark landings.

But the marathon heightened when Tommy learned that all shop owners closed their businesses in Monrovia for a two-hour siesta every day. Between noon and two o'clock, it was impossible to find a single store open for business. Abijoudi proved to be very helpful, even irreplaceable, in expediting business required for our mission, even during the siesta times. Meetings prearranged by Abijoudi for Tommy's time in Monrovia proved to be more than just helpful—they were absolutely necessary.

While Tommy and Abijoudi carried on their business, I sat holding my bottle of Coca- Cola, gazing into the mélange of culture and people across the bustling street. People wore long, flowing robes, while some wore turbans and others wore tasseled fezzes. But the "country" people (locals) of Liberia intrigued me the most. Their native dresses were vibrant, colorful, designs splashed with a brilliance that mesmerized me. I sat transfixed as they paraded by me. It was as if their colorful fashion show were just for my enjoyment. Whoever had dyed their cloth was certainly NOT afraid to use color. I LOVED their unique artistry and the bold, colorful dyes!

In that same moment I saw something that made me laugh. Across the road and beyond a few feet stood a little lean-to shanty. It appeared to have been made of odds and ends of metal scraps, carefully and proudly nailed together. One entire wall of the shanty was made from a single metal sign. At one time the sign had been an advertisement for Tide soap. Resting in its place in its former splendor, the sign still displayed some of its bright orange and red colors. By now the sign was a little faded and the white stripes were rusted. But it was still readable and serviceable for the owner's particular use as a wall.

That day God showed me that, even in Africa, Tide soap and Coca-Cola were available to me for my use and enjoyment. For some people, having those two things available to them may not have been important. But I smiled as I realized God had given these special gifts to me. I felt quite comforted in having something familiar from my own culture.

Living in Africa was beginning to feel a little more like home all the time. When Tommy and I left our home and families in Houston, Texas to move to Africa, we thought we had left behind everything familiar to us. But God showed me that day, via a Tide soap sign and a bottle of Coca-Cola, that no matter how diverse our cultures, there were still commonalities. Something so simple and so unexpected had become very comforting to me. And I knew with God's help, we would be just fine in our new home and new country.

Hebrews 11:1 (NIV)

"Now faith is being sure of what we hope for and certain of what we do not see."

CHAPTER 2
The Dumpling

I'm a southerner and was newly married to a handsome, young, missionary pilot. We had just moved to Liberia. One of my first realizations upon arriving in Africa was how grateful I was that we didn't have to live in a grass hut. Instead, we lived in prefab housing. I even had an electric stove and a refrigerator. However, I was in great need of learning how to cook for my new husband. Consequently, the stove and I were about to become intimately acquainted. Being almost 18 years old, I was determined my youth would not hinder my ability to learn to cook nor hamper me in learning to do anything else.

Since we had left home in the States, there was one thing I craved—my mom's chicken and dumplings. Although meat in general was scarce in Africa, our mission did raise chickens for their meat and eggs. And chicken and eggs were the two things I knew how to cook! But my problem was that none of my cookbooks had recipes for the type of dumplings my mom had made. My only recourse was to write my mother for her wonderful recipe. I wrote her and religiously waited for the plane to arrive with our mail. I could hardly wait to receive my mom's dumpling recipe. But it took almost two months before receiving a response from her.

The day mom's letter arrived I went to see Johnnie Weah. Johnnie was the African guy in charge of Tournata's chickens. I asked him to catch, kill, pluck and gut a chicken for me. Life was not simple living in a third-world country and neither was learning to cook there. But I was dripping with enthusiasm about cooking mom's dish. After months of waiting for mom's recipe, I had worked up a hearty appetite for her special chicken and dumplings! Maybe the fact that I was "expecting" had a little to do with my cravings for that dish as well. I had even begun to dream about those sumptuous chicken and dumplings!

But you know moms! They've cooked for so many years that rarely do they measure anything anymore! She had written on her recipe a "pinch" of this and a "dab" of that. Mom forgot that her inexperienced and unlearned daughter knew NOTHING about pinches and dabs. I'm sure she remembered the numerous times I had watched her make the dumplings. She assumed that I would remember how she made them, step by step. The truth was that I'd forgotten one very important step in making those dumplings. And she forgot to mention that in her recipe. I was supposed to add the dumplings one at a time to the pot of bubbling broth.

I brought a huge pot of broth to a boil on the electric stove. I had remembered that step correctly. The next step in my instructions was, "Add the rolled-out dumplings to the boiling broth." AND I did just that—ALL at one time!

After I dropped all the rolled-out dumplings into the broth, that huge pot of bubbling broth suddenly got very still and quiet. All of those dumplings had sucked every drop of broth from that huge pot. What I saw in that pot in no way, shape, or form resembled my mom's chicken and dumplings. Instead, there was only one, huge dumpling glued to the inside of the pot! I gasped at the poor, pitiful, pale mass! When I tried to remove it, the huge mass refused to come out of the pot. I turned that pot upside down onto a very large platter. The mass of dumpling shimmied and shook as if it were something alive. I was humiliated and embarrassed as Tommy and I sat down to eat our long-awaited chicken and dumplings. He had been almost as excited about the recipe as I had been. And now, there it sat, quivering and quaking on the platter. Tommy, who was well aware of my limited cooking skills, was sorely tested on that day. He picked up his knife and fork, pointed at the quivering pale mass, and said to me, "Slice me off a hunk of that!"

Both of us began to laugh and we laughed until we cried. I cried because of my embarrassment and failure in preparing our long-awaited dinner. He cried with me because I was so upset. Had he not handled the situation with such humor and compassion, it would have been my worst nightmare! We laughed together about my mistake and then we got on with our lives.

The wonderful thing in remembering the "dumpling disaster" was that Tommy never once mentioned it to anyone. I've told this story about myself many times, but not Tommy. I loved him very much for that. It made me want to try all the more to be the best cook and wife that I could be for him.

Proverbs 15:23

*"A man has joy in an apt answer,
and how delightful is a timely answer."*

1 Corinthians 13:4

*"Love suffers long and is kind...
and does not behave rudely..."*

CHAPTER 3
Rain, Corks and Snakes

For a kid who grew up deep in the heart of Texas, I found it unusual that I was so fascinated with a place so far away called Africa. Because of my very early interest, I continually scoured our school library in tiny Shepherd, Texas to read and learn all that I could about that continent. The animals in particular were of great interest to me. Growing up on a farm, there was little that I feared, except snakes; I hated snakes!

On the Tournata mission, our prefab houses were made of two modular sections connected by a hall and bathroom. Two bedrooms comprised one section and a kitchen/living area was in the other. There was a three-inch step-over between the bedroom and hall and another one between the hall and living room. This arrangement created some unusual problems living in West Africa. There was also a refrigerator and electric range in the kitchen similar to one you might find in the States. And that was our home.

One of the things I loved most about Africa was the rain; I love rain! But rain in Liberia was unlike any I'd ever seen before! I was from Houston, Texas where a lot of rain was a common and regular occurrence. But the rains we had in Liberia were far more plentiful than those in Houston. Thirteen inches of rain in one afternoon was not uncommon where we lived along the coast in Liberia. However, no water stood in puddles anywhere afterwards. God is so incredibly creative in making every place in the world able to compensate for its own peculiarities.

The first time we had a huge rainstorm, the hall/bathroom sections of our home filled with water because of the three- inch step-over. Consequently, I had to wear rubber boots when walking through these areas. The boots kept my feet warm and dry and kept me from being electrocuted when I used my electric stove. On previous occasions I had received an electrical shock while cooking during the damp, rainy season.

Tournata's carpenter was an African named Lee Jobba (JOB ah). One day I went to him and asked to borrow a "brace and bit." I had an idea. Lee smiled, perhaps because he was surprised that I even knew what a brace and bit was. Since my grandfather had been a carpenter, I had grown up around tools. He had taught me that a brace and bit was useful for drilling holes in wood.

I was ecstatic about my idea. I almost ran back to our house with that brace and bit clasped to my chest. You would have thought it was some priceless treasure that I'd discovered. But the old, familiar adage proved to be true—necessity WAS the mother of invention!

Immediately I went to the hall/bathroom area with that brace and bit in hand and I began to put my idea into action. I drilled holes in the floor so that the water could drain out. I must admit that I was quite pleased with my own ingenuity. The other plus for me was that it would solve the problem of getting shocked when the electric stove was in use. But there was one small detail I had not considered or even processed—snakes!

Green and black mamba snakes were very common in our area. Although they are usually quite long, they are also very small in diameter. Unfortunately, now they would have easy access into our home via the drilled holes in the floor! The holes I had so ecstatically and laboriously drilled through the floor had now become a potential nightmare. I was crestfallen and more than a little ashamed of my hasty decision.

Instantly a solution sprang into my thoughts! Corks! What I needed was corks to plug the holes! There at Tournata I went from missionary to missionary and asked for corks.

Returning home, I placed the corks into the holes. The next time it rained and the room began to fill with water, I simply pulled out the corks, allowing the water to drain out. My problem was solved.

Proverbs 15:33

*"The fear of the Lord is the instruction for wisdom,
and before honor comes humility."*

CHAPTER 4
Terror in the Sky

Living in Africa was a dream come true for me. Africa had been a place I had always longed to see! That foreign continent had fascinated me. I had read a lot about its exotic animals, thick, dense jungle, and blue/black-skinned people. And at last I was there. The word exciting can't begin to describe my thoughts or emotions! Yet, we had no idea of the experiences and challenges that lay ahead for the two of us. Some of those challenges would make life for my husband and me more than adventuresome; they were downright scary!

Being a bush pilot in Africa sounded exciting and it was for Tommy. But certain aspects of his occupation vacillated between being hilarious and horrendous. His job required him to fly into Monrovia, the capital city, at least once a week. Several tasks had to be accomplished on those weekly trips: delivering eggs to Radio Station ELWA (Eternal Love Winning Africa), retrieving all the mail and packages, obtaining parts for engines and being the general "gopher" for all who needed anything. Almost everyone at Tournata required something from Monrovia at one time or another. Before leaving for Monrovia, there would be a line of ladies with their lists of things for Tommy to obtain, time permitting. At times those items could be as simple as a spool of thread or air-letter forms purchased from Monrovia's municipal post office. Only a few people would be at the strip when Tommy left for Monrovia, but everyone was there when he returned. The reason? MAIL. We were all ecstatic to receive letters from our loved one's back home!

One gray Sunday afternoon Tommy and I prepared to fly out of Tournata to Monrovia. That particular day the sky looked like a watercolor painting gone amok. The gray of the sky and sea appeared to run together. It was not a pretty sight.

It was my first trip into the big city of Monrovia since our arrival five months earlier. I was more than ready for some "R & R," at least as much as a gal who was five months pregnant could enjoy. Even though my husband was the pilot and a licensed flight instructor, still I was not comfortable flying in bad weather. I noticed the gray skies had changed to a light drizzle. I looked inquiringly at Tommy, but he assured me that we would be okay. He was a good pilot and I trusted him to get us there safely. We boarded the plane and taxied down the strip for our take-off. It was customary for the pilot to turn and fly back over the mission after taking off and we did that.

Soon we were airborne and on our way to enjoy our first overnight together in Monrovia. One concern had been leaving our mission station without a pilot on hand. Something could happen that would require a pilot to fly one of the missionaries out. But our flight was only about an hour and 10 minutes long. AND we did have a ham-radio session scheduled with Tournata the following morning. We felt at peace about the trip to Monrovia. Weather was always a factor for pilots to consider. But their decision-making often depended on the seasons. We were in between our two regular seasons. The two seasons in Liberia were either hot and rainy or cool and rainy (the latter was also called "dry season"). Dry season meant less rain than the normal times. The disturbing thing about "in-between season" weather was that it could change in a flash and it usually did. The storms occurring during those times could be unpredictable and violent.

Tommy and I were flying along the normal route to Monrovia. We followed the rules that stated that a pilot flying TO Monrovia (going west) must fly over the bush. But returning FROM Monrovia (going east), he must fly over the water. Even the local airlines, such as Liberian National Airlines, flew their DC-3s adhering to that rule. In addition, almost all flights were daytime flights. The reason was because the airports, except Robert's field and Monrovia's field, had no landing lights for take-offs or landings after dark. Pilots in Liberia, regardless of their experience or credentials, were considered "fair-weather flyers." They may have all of their ratings for instrument flying, but without airfields equipped with runway lights, planes could not safely land. Simply put—no landing lights, no flights! And furthermore, pilots needed to know the exact time the sun would set; they HAD to be down and out of the sky before dark!

The rain was becoming more intense and the turbulence nastier by the minute. Tommy asked me to tighten my seatbelt; I was getting bounced around too much. Even with my seatbelt fastened as tightly as possible, the top of my head was still hitting the metal roof of the Cessna-195.

Tommy standing by Cessna - 195

The Cessna was an aluminum, single-engine prop plane. Normally, it would seat five people. But the back seat had been removed to allow space for crates of eggs and other cargo. Above my head was the plexi-glas windshield of the plane; metal rivets held it in place. The rivet directly over me was leaking rainwater. With my fingernail, I tried to screw the rivet tighter to keep the water from dripping on me. It was hopeless, but I continued trying since it kept my hands and mind occupied. I tried not to dwell on the raging storm and increasing violence exploding outside the plane. Lightning was everywhere and the plane was pitching about like a rodeo bull. Up we went and then down again! There was no "flying straight and level" on that day!

At one point, Tommy decided to fly under the storm. But at almost treetop level, we were dangerously close to being slammed into the bush below us. Next he attempted to go above the storm, but there the storm was even worse.

By that time, I was definitely a "white-knuckler." My eyes were glued to the instrument panel in front of me.

Back when Tommy and I were dating, he had given me several flying lessons in case I ever needed to fly. I had logged about 20 hours, but I had never "soloed!" Since Tommy was the only pilot on our mission station, there was concern about his being gone, leaving two pregnant missionaries without an available pilot. Carolyn Morgret and I were those two ladies. The possibility of an emergency flight had to be considered. I prayed that I would never have to fly anyone out of Tournata. Tournata did have two planes: a small four-passenger Piper Pacer and the five-passenger Cessna-195. Both were single-engine planes, but the Pacer was smaller and similar to the plane I had learned to fly.

By now, the sounds and noises of the storm had become alarming to me. I wondered what was happening to our aluminum plane. The noise was deafening! I could hear the metal rivets popping and straining loudly. The plane creaked and groaned while we were being tossed about inside. I managed to have enough control over my senses not to cause Tommy any other distractions. I believe that plane ride was my greatest test in exercising self-control. Tommy needed his undivided attention on the instrument panel to try to keep us in the air! BUT I prayed that day aloud to God! And oh, how I prayed!

Lightning continued to bounce off both wings of the plane. Suddenly, the plane was totally out of control and we began to flip end-over-end before spiraling downward. Once again, I kept my thoughts to myself and prayed that God would give back control of the plane to Tommy.

The violence of the storm had wrenched it from him. For reasons unknown to him, Tommy could not MAKE the plane respond to his commands!

Our situation was perilous! The plane continued its twisting, turning and spiraling downward toward the angry, black, foaming sea. I thought, "Ginger, you and Tommy are going to die and you will never see or hold your baby!" At last (it seemed forever), Tommy was able to bring the plane back under his control.

After we leveled out, only six feet separated our plane's wheels from the furiously foaming, black sea. I turned in my seat to look back at the storm, trying to get a visual of what we had just encountered. Never before or since have I seen such a horrible sight!

Both the sky and the water were purplish-black with yellow green tones. It was impossible to tell where the sky ended and the sea began. Only the white caps told me where the sea was. The roiling white caps almost splashed against the wheels of the plane. But we were able to gain enough altitude to finally get us out of harm's way.

Isaiah 14:24

"...Surely, just as I have intended so it has happened, and just as I have planned so it will stand."

Both Tommy and I were silent for the remainder of our trip into Monrovia. After we had landed, we got out of the plane and stood leaning against the plane. Words were not necessary as we silently hugged each other. Before we left Tournata, we had made plans for that evening to go to dinner in Monrovia and then go to a movie. Instead, Tommy ordered room service for us in our hotel. We spent the evening talking quietly about our near-death experience, our unborn child and our hopes and plans for our future. At least for now, we had a future.

Jeremiah 29:11

"For I know the plans I have for you," declares the Lord, "plans for welfare and not for calamity, to give you a future and a hope."

CHAPTER 5
When Not to Shoot a Crocodile

I know that living in Africa and being married to a pilot sounds romantic. But as we later discovered, there would be numerous challenges in that romance thing!

We lived along the coast on the edge of Baffu Bay. It was a little like living in Hawaii with palm trees and sandy beaches, only the people had blue-black skin. The beaches, although not huge, were very pretty. And if you walked along the beach at night barefoot, sparks would fly up from the sand. When we examined the sand, it contained dark grains of something. I suspect that those dark grains were the reason for the sparks; carbon maybe? We weren't sure exactly what it was but was very unique and interesting to me.

But the best thing about the beach was going to sleep at night to the sound of waves breaking on the shore; it was almost idyllic.

A few months into our two-year term, it became evident to me that flying over the bush in a small plane was not hazardous or adventurous enough for Tommy. The fact that he took up elephant hunting, snorkeling, skin-diving and water-skiing (on the same river he hunted crocodiles) proves my point. Since that river was very near our house, Tommy had ample opportunity to pursue his adventures. When adapting to a new culture, climate and country, it is easy to find new adventures or hobbies to experience in one's free time.

Tommy's parents came to visit us six weeks after our daughter Vicki was born. It was their first grandchild and, for them, Africa was not too far away from Texas to travel to meet her. We were really happy to see them.

One evening, Tommy and his dad, along with our Liberian helper Sammy, and I climbed into one of the available dugout canoes. Like most canoes, they were not very stable in the water; at times even breathing made them sway. We waited for it to become dark and until the tide was going in the right direction. Finally, when everything was right we paddled furiously down the dark and dangerous river. I considered yelling, as Tarzan did in the movies, but I restrained myself.

The undergrowth on both sides of the river had not been a problem until we got farther down where the river narrowed. Then tangled vines and overgrowth made the river appear to be a very dark and long tunnel. We had all kinds of stuff growing over our heads and hanging down over us. Occasionally it was necessary to duck our heads to keep from getting strangled by the trailing vines and branches. I couldn't help but wonder what kind of hairy, horrible creature or humongous snake was hiding above us in that tangle of brush and vines. With my vivid imagination on a rampage, it was difficult to stay calm; more than my palms were sweating by that time.

We had brought some battery-operated lights with us to shine along the riverbanks. Tommy was told that when the spotlights were reflected on the eyes of the crocodiles, they would glow a very bright red! Also, we had brought along a pistol and a gig, similar to one a person might use for gigging frogs. What I knew about either of those items you could put on a pinhead and still have room to write The Declaration of Independence or at least my obituary.

Soon we came upon a beautiful (Tommy's words) pair of glowing, red eyes and Tommy shot the crocodile. Assuming it to be dead, we moved closer so that Tommy and Sammy could gig the crocodile and wrestle it into our dugout. The unstable dugout began swaying back and forth as my father-in-law and I tried to keep it from tipping over. "Surely," I thought, "we are going to capsize!" AND, to add to the growing list of hazards, I couldn't swim! At last the crocodile was pulled inside the dugout WITH us. Panting with exhaustion, the guys collapsed and tried to catch their breath.

At that point, it was difficult to see who won: the inexperienced guys or the wily crocodile. It wasn't exactly the smell of victory that they exhibited, but the defeated foe lay bleeding in our dugout. Suddenly, that dugout came alive with the activity of one very much alive, thrashing and angry crocodile. The bloody crocodile was whipping its tail and head around while the dugout heaved violently. I did the one thing that I thought was appropriate for such a moment: I screamed like a Banshee! It became obvious to me that one miserable, supposedly dead crocodile was going to send the four of us into the river where the remaining members of his family lived. I was certain that we would become their late- night snack.

Amidst all of the confusion and with the crocodile thrashing around in the already unstable and too small dugout, I gave Tommy some advice that he chose not to take! I yelled to Tommy, who was carrying the only pistol, "Shoot him! Shoot him!" Tommy calmly replied, "Yeah, if I shoot him in the dugout, it will put a hole in it and then we will have a much bigger problem." At last they were able to gig the crocodile a second time.

Once again, they held him out over the side of the dugout and shot him! That time the crocodile stayed dead!

In spite of some frightening moments, we arrived safely back at Tournata with only a few battle scars from the floundering crocodile's tail. But we all had our own version of that eventful night's drama. One thing has remained the same for me—I've never wanted to go crocodile hunting again!

During stressful times such as the croc hunt, my imagination goes into overdrive and begins to spit out images of headlines that might have appeared in the Houston Chronicle. It would have read something like this: "Missionary and Wife Presumed Eaten by Crocs."

On a lighter note, the rumor among the missionaries was that crocodile meat was quite edible and tasty. Since meat was in very short supply, even crocodile meat would have been a welcome addition to our limited diet. But aside from that, we thought maybe Tommy's dad, a pastor, and his mom would enjoy eating something else that tasted like chicken.

In retrospect, there are times when a husband should NOT listen to his hysterical wife! That was definitely one of those times!

Proverbs 21:23

"He who guards his mouth and his tongue, guards his soul from troubles."

CHAPTER 6
The Day of the Driver Ant Invasion

For missionaries, living with or around the unusual becomes the norm. It became interesting as well for those of us new to another culture and country. There was the heat, the humidity, the strange insects, snakes and things that go "bump in the night." Some of those are worth checking out and quickly. But one of the most unusual sights I ever saw happened on a beautiful, sunny, Saturday afternoon within our Tournata mission compound. The year was 1959.

With Tommy as the pilot, five of the six men from Tournata boarded our mission's Cessna-195. They flew to a government event that was by invitation only (translation—you MUST attend)! Max Lange, the only man left at Tournata, was very ill with malaria. That left only the women and about a bazillion kids on the Tournata compound. But unknown to us at that moment, there were about 50 bazillion driver ants also.

Driver ants are only found in Africa. They are VERY interesting insects and differ from army ants found in many other countries. Army ants have a venomous bite. Their bite can cause the bitten tissue to liquefy, making it more digestible for the army ant. But driver ants have very powerful mandibles, which can slice into their victims, making it possible for the ants to eat their prey. There could be as many as 100,000 sister ants in a swarm, working as a single hunting unit. They are "swarm-raiders" and hunt above the ground.

Driver "guard" ants form triple rows on the outer edges of their paths and stand on their hind legs guarding the swarm- raiders. Like other ants, driver ants are very industrious, with each ant having specific duties to perform. They do NOTHING without the queen's permission. Driver ants have been known to kill pigs, chickens, goats, cows or even humans unaware of their presence, especially the blind, babies or the in-firmed.

Almost immediately after the Cessna-195 took off with all our men on board, the driver ant problem became apparent near one of the missionary's homes. Driver ants always occur in large numbers. It has been recorded that their path can be as much as 50 feet wide and easily spotted from the air. In such large numbers, they can give the appearance of a black, paved road but having erratic boundaries. If you have ever been to Africa, you would know that in the "bush country" there are no blacktopped roads! Because our colony of ants had not yet developed into that blacktop look, they went unnoticed by our men in the air.

One of the nationals came running to me and said, "We have big problems; driver ants are here." Previously, someone had mentioned the use of fuel oil to rid oneself of the pesky ants. Fuel oil was a mixture of oil and fuel, very much like diesel, that our mission used to run our generator. If fuel oil were poured onto the ants, that would resolve our problems; at least, that was what we had heard.

Those of us who were hale and hearty began our trek to the aviation barn to get the fuel oil in buckets. We returned as quickly as we could to pour the oily, black gunk onto the marauding ants.

I can only say that idea may have looked good on paper but in reality the determined ants seemed to be invigorated by the fuel oil. Since "plan A" with the fuel oil had not worked, "plan B" was put into action. I suggested, instead of the impotent fuel oil, we should switch to aviation fuel. Aviation fuel is very high in octane and extremely volatile. I thought we should "kick it up a notch" by soaking them in aviation fuel and then lighting them on fire. The only problem with that idea was that we could literally become "a light unto the world" if we came too close. But our backs were against the wall with the masses of driver ants gathering momentum by the minute.

While we were pondering whether to set fire to the ants, the ants were not calmly sitting on the sidelines awaiting our decision. Their number seemed to multiply as they began their "divide-and-conquer" plan. Upon discovering the ants were traveling in the direction of the Knowles' home, my friend Carol and I decided we HAD to do something and quickly. Even more ants were close to the Tournata office as well. Since all of our houses were prefab set on ten-foot poles, the ants had begun crawling up the poles. By this time, they were entering the Knowles' home. We were frantic to do something immediately!

Carol and I soaked the long, black, shimmering line of driver ants with aviation fuel, telling everyone, "Stand back, WAY back." Then Carol lit the match and tossed it upon the mass of ants. In a huge puff of smoke and a noise that might have equaled a sonic boom, the long line of ants was annihilated. Our blessing was that neither the ants nor the staggering blast caused by the aviation fuel consumed us that day. But I must admit, I had not expected such a violent explosion. I had expected some kind of noise, but NOTHING like the sound we heard that day.

We had been told that the only way to rid oneself of driver ants was to find the queen and dispose of her. After she was destroyed, all the other ants would disband until the ants chose a new queen. Meanwhile, some of the nationals had started their own search for the driver ant queen. Soon they found her and her size amazed us. She was as large as the palm of a man's hand. Everyone rejoiced over finding the queen. After she was destroyed, we would have no further problems with driver ants.

When our men returned from the government event, they had several conversations about the safety issues involved if there were any future problems with driver ants. It was decided that aviation fuel was a little too expensive and explosive for killing ants. But considering everything, the men were proud that we took charge and solved our "antsy" problem.

Proverbs 12:13b

"...the righteous will escape from trouble."

CHAPTER 7
Living Out Ecclesiastes Chapter 3

Except for my dad's military service in Panama, my family had never traveled outside the U. S. So when Tommy, my fiancé, asked me what I thought about living in Africa, I was excited and overjoyed! It seemed that my childhood dreams of seeing Africa was about to come true.

Tommy and I were married in April 1957. In mid-June, we flew to West Africa and deplaned at Robert's Field in Liberia. Years before, the United States had used Robert's Field as a military base during WW II. It was there that we spent our first night in Liberia in those old converted army barracks made into a quasi-hotel. I expected to hear elephants trumpeting or lions roaring in the night! But I was sorely disappointed. Due to complete exhaustion from two days of air-travel, I instantly fell fast asleep and heard NOTHING! Later, I would discover that lions did not live in Liberia, but elephants were plentiful!

"A Time to Laugh"

R. G. LeTourneau had two missions. One was in Lima, Peru and the other was in Liberia, West Africa; Tommy was the pilot for the Liberian mission. After our arrival, we were overjoyed to be living at Tournata. There we began to establish our home, our family and our lives together. We could not have been happier.

"A Time To Heal"

A year or so later, Tommy became very ill. He was diagnosed (via ham radio) by a physician in Monrovia and was told that he had malaria. Two weeks later, I too became very ill with the same symptoms. Too weak to walk, I was carried to the plane to seek medical help at Pleebo's Firestone Hospital. Pleebo was a 75-minute flight down the coast and inland. Landing on the Pleebo airstrip was a nightmare on the best of days. The strip was too short, uphill and it had a bridge to maneuver over. The bridge was at the bottom of that grassy hill they gratuitously called a runway. The pilot needed to set the plane's wheels onto the bridge first or the plane would overshoot the runway. An incorrect landing would send the plane down into a deep ravine. As a reminder, there was a graveyard of planes strewn about in the ravine below. Very few pilots attempted to land at Pleebo. Most pilots opted for the larger strip at the Cape Palmas airfield. But that was still an hour's drive from Pleebo. I was too ill for the drive; consequently, we landed on the Pleebo airstrip.

Immediately upon arriving at the Firestone Hospital, doctors diagnosed me with infectious hepatitis. They also discovered I was in the early stages of pregnancy. The doctors and Tommy made the decision that I would take Vicki, our one-year-old, and fly to the States as soon as I was strong enough to travel. I did not want to go AND I did not want to leave Tommy in Africa! I tried every conceivable way to convince Tommy to allow me to stay, but to no avail. Near the end of January, Vicki and I flew out of Africa to Houston.

"A Time to Give Birth"

Following the birth of our son in August 1959, Tommy left the three of us and flew back to Monrovia. We would be living there since our tenure with LeTourneau was complete. While I was still in Houston, Tommy had accepted another flying job for a "bush airline" called Datco Airlines. The term bush airline simply meant the pilot would be flying to remote bush strips rather than to the larger airfields. Liberian National Airlines (LNA) flew their DC-3s to larger cities with bigger and better runways. But even flying on LNA planes, your seating companion might be a goat or a crate of chickens. LNA was rustic at best. The need for an airline to fly people into the smaller villages was critical. But landing there required that the smaller planes be able to land on the tiny airstrips. Tommy's primary purpose for flying for such an airline was to accrue multi-engine hours. He had thousands of hours in single engine planes because he had owned his own plane and he had been a flight instructor for single-engine planes. By logging many multi engine hours, upon our return to the States Tommy could apply to fly for an airline or for some corporation as their private pilot. Those were our plans for the future.

Jeremiah 29:11

"I know the plans I have for you, plans for good and not for evil; to give you a future and a hope."

"A Time to Search"

Before I could leave Houston though, Tommy needed to find a home for us in Monrovia and quickly. The anticipation of being together again was the impetus I needed for boarding KLM (Royal Dutch Airlines) and flying with our six-week-old son and 20- month-old daughter ALONE. The trip without children tested one's physical limitations. But traveling with two babies, with necessary stops in Montreal, Amsterdam, Lisbon and Dakar in the Senegal Republic of northwest Africa, would be utterly exhausting for the three of us. Yet, it was something I had to do. With Vicki and Randy in tow, I boarded our KLM flight in Houston prepared as well as one could be for the 30-hour journey ahead of us. Looking and feeling like the "Wreck of the Hesperus," we arrived at last in Monrovia in late September. Our reunion was beyond description. We were a family once again and, at last, living together on the same continent!

The house Tommy had found for us was located on Bush Rod Island. A short bridge connected the island to Monrovia and was easily accessible by car. It was a huge house and, because of its size, we divided it into two separate living facilities. Our family lived downstairs while Datco pilot Duane Marvin and his wife Charlotte occupied the upstairs floor. The upstairs had its own modern kitchen with pink appliances and black granite counter tops. The house at one time had been a single-family home. It was WAY too big for our family of four, but it was ideal to share with the Marvins. And since Tommy and Duane both flew for Datco, they could ride to work together!

"A Time to Love"

As a family, we had been attending church services at radio station ELWA. The station was located outside Monrovia in the countryside. Fellow-shipping with other Christians blessed us, encouraged us and gave us a sense of belonging in Liberia. It also allowed our children to learn to play with children their own age. Sophie and Ray de la Haye from Canada were managers of ELWA and our personal friends. We had met them when they vacationed at Tournata two years earlier. Instantly Tommy and I fell in love with them.

The de la Hayes had children past their teen years and they became the parent figures Tommy and I needed while living in Liberia. God had begun to surround us with encouraging and supportive Christians such as Ray and Sophie. And the time was drawing near when God would use them mightily in my life.

"An Appointed Time for Everything"

The manager at Tournata and our close friend Walt Knowles came to Monrovia on business. He stayed overnight with us and we were late getting to bed. We were trying to catch up on all the news from Tournata. Hearing all about our friends and their news was like a breath of fresh air for us. We missed our friends at Tournata.

It was a Thursday morning, the seventh of April. I cooked breakfast for all of us and Walt left to attend business in town. Because I ran late that morning, I didn't have time to make Tommy's lunch before dropping him off at the airfield. Around ten o'clock that morning, I drove to the airfield to take his lunch to him, but I missed seeing him because he had taken an earlier flight. The mechanic's wife Roberta (Berta) Dodge lived not far from the airport; I decided to drop by to visit with her. They had just leased a pretty, little, yellow bungalow very near the Monrovia airfield. It was the perfect time to spend a few minutes with Berta before returning to the airfield to give Tommy his lunch.

But Tommy had left on a chartered flight to the diamond mines and to a tiny airstrip called Weeswa (WEES wah). Tommy and Tom O'Dell, a guy from Brooklyn, New York, were the only two Datco pilots allowed to fly there. Flying to the diamond mines required special clearance and only Tommy and Tom had the government's permission to take off and land there.

The Weeswa strip was okay for landing in an STOL (single engine take-off and landing) plane, but take-offs there were an ever-present danger. The strip was shaped like a walking cane. The pilots would start their take-offs on the 'crook' part of the strip; then they would swing the plane around to have more distance for take-off. There was another problem, though. During take-off, fuel shifted in the wings. That caused the plane's engine to pause at the most critical time in the take-off. In that critical moment, the pilots could only pray the plane's engine would "catch" with enough fuel to become airborne; that was their hope. Earlier in January, Tommy's engine did NOT respond in time with enough fuel and he crashed. But he lived to tell about it and walked away from the crash with only minor bruises, plus a deep cut on his forehead. I do believe God used that crash to prepare me emotionally for what lay ahead for me.

After Tommy's crash at Weeswa, Joe Dodge, the Datco mechanic, devised an effective solution for the fuel-starved engine problem. He installed an auxiliary fuel tank. The new tank allowed a continual flow of fuel into the engine. The problem of the nightmarish take-offs at Weeswa was solved!

Meanwhile, as I visited with Berta, Tommy returned from Weeswa and changed from his single-engine plane to a twin engine plane for yet another flight. Tom O'Dell had just flown the twin craft from a mountainous area; he didn't even shut down the engines. It was Tom's plane that Tommy boarded for his next flight.

Tommy in the Piper Apache "A Time for Every Event Under Heaven"

Major Dunne, Datco's manager, always stood outside his office in view of the runway and watched every one of his pilot's take-offs. On that day, both Major and Tom stood watching Tommy as he taxied to the end of the runway to check out the twin-engine Piper Apache plane. The normal procedure for every take-off, whether or not the engine(s) had ever been shut down, was to check out the engines. Because Tom had left both engines running, my Tommy boarded the plane, taxied to the end of the runway and checked out the engines/instruments before he took off.

While Major and Tom watched Tommy take off, both had noticed white smoke billowing out of one of the engines. His plane was only six feet off the tarmac and, at that moment, a split- second decision HAD to be made. By now, the smoking engine had died. In a situation like that, a pilot has only two options:

1. Set the plane down immediately or
2. Proceed with the flight, but bring the plane back immediately to be checked out. Tommy decided on the second option, even though the plane had the capability of flying fully loaded on one engine. In addition, the plane was totally empty since he had not yet picked up his clients for this chartered flight. Tom and Major saw Tommy "feather the prop" of the dead engine and make his turn toward the good-engine side of the plane. It was apparent that Tommy was attempting to return the aircraft for Datco's mechanic Joe to inspect the dead engine. He had performed exactly the correct maneuver under these circumstances. There was no reason for him to think that he would be at risk bringing the plane back around to be checked out. But standing in the way of Tommy's safe return to the runway was a lone palm tree. Then the second engine failed. The plane hit the tree and dropped like a rock.

"A Time to Die"

It's strange to me that I can't remember who came to Berta's to tell me Tommy had crashed. I believe it was

Zara, Major's wife. But whoever it was took me to the local hospital where Tommy had been taken. My mind was awhirl with thoughts I didn't want to acknowledge; they were too painful to process. Strangely though, I do remember climbing stairs to the second floor of the hospital where the surgical unit was located.

And I remember thinking that someone should replace the cracked and dirty linoleum covering those stairs. As I walked down the corridor, I paused a moment and looked out the hospital window. In a flash, a conversation I had with my mom years before exploded into my thoughts. I must have been 10 or 11 years old when our conversation took place. But the scene was as fresh in my memory as if it had happened yesterday. Mom and I stood side-by side washing fruit jars one very hot, summer day; Mom was canning jelly. She turned to me and said, "Virginia, I want you to always remember this; God will never give you more than you can bear." In that moment as I stood in that hospital corridor, God brought her words back to me. As a young and inexperienced Christian, God had just prepared me for what was about to take place in my life! And He was going to use the essence of a Scripture to do it! Years later, I would discover the Scripture stating those same words my mother had spoken to me years before. The verse is:

1 Corinthians 10:13

"No temptation has overtaken you but such as is common to man; and God is faithful, who will not allow you to be tempted beyond what you are able, but with the temptation will

*provide the way to escape also, that you may
be able to endure it."*

Just a couple of minutes after God had prepared my heart using Mom's admonition, the doctor appeared down the corridor and walked toward me. I knew by his body language that his news was not good. Behind the doctor, I had caught a glimpse of Walt Knowles hurrying to get to me. Walt arrived just as the doctor said to me, "He didn't make it."

They were only four words, ordinary words, words we use every day in conversation, but in different contexts. Yet, those words had the power to alter my life completely and forever. I felt as if my own life had been sucked right out of my body; I couldn't even breathe as I tried to assimilate that awful news.

Later, someone put me in a taxi to take me to our Bush Rod Island home. Going there, I was appalled to see that everything in the area looked strange and foreign to me; not a single thing looked familiar. It was as though someone had plucked me from all that was familiar to me in Monrovia and set me down in Outer Mongolia, Timbuktu or some other place I had never been before! That sense of strangeness only added to my despair and sadness.

"A Time to Weep"

But I was able to see God's faithfulness to me in having Walt Knowles in Monrovia on business. He rarely ever left Tournata to come to Monrovia. But God knew that I would need Walt and he was there! Walt, a former pastor, sat down with me and walked me through scriptures and events. He was able to comfort me, helping me to see God's faithfulness to me even in Tommy's death. Walt reminded me that the most important thing was that Tommy belonged to the Lord. And he was with HIM now; I knew that! But I needed to hear Walt say those words to me again. Another major blessing was that no one else was killed in the crash.

Ecclesiastes 3:11b

"…He has also set eternity in their heart, yet so that man will not find out the work which God has done from the beginning even to the end."

I was 20 years old, but I felt as though I were a hundred. The huge responsibility for our two-year-old, Vicki, and Randy, our eight-month-old, lay heavily upon me. I wondered how we could possibly live without Tommy. Our third anniversary was still 12 days away! Early in our marriage Tommy had begun talking with me about what I should do if he crashed and did not survive. I remember crying and not wanting to think about that possibility at the time. Yet, I knew flying was hazardous and especially in Africa. If some problem should arise, there's no pulling over to the curb or lifting the hood to repair the plane. Often, Tommy and I laughed about his trying to find a soft tree if such a need should occur. I knew there were risks! But even knowing them, I was not prepared for his death. It changed everything in my life. It even changed me; I was no longer his wife, no longer his partner or companion! The precious husband and loving dad was no longer there for us.

Then another thought came to me. How could I possibly leave Africa? I knew I must, but I didn't see how I could do that. I felt as though my life was over, done, finished! I felt very alone, even abandoned. There was such a flood of emotions and thoughts. He was dead, yet I still felt very married to him. Much later, I would find that thought still haunting me. Now the word "future" mocked me and held nothing of interest for me, especially without Tommy in my life.

Psalm 27:13-14

> *"I would have despaired unless I would have believed that I would see the goodness of the Lord in the land of the living. Wait for the Lord; be strong and let your heart take courage; yes, wait for the Lord."*

"A Time to Mourn"

Amid my grief, there were goodbyes to be said; I've never been very good with doing that under normal circumstances. I knew I would never see some of our friends and acquaintances again. Some of them were from all parts of the world. One by one they began to drop by our home to say their goodbyes to me. Life for me and for my children had spun completely out of control. At that point I had only one plan and that was to fly to Houston as soon as arrangements could be made after Tommy's

Liberian memorial service. After that, I had NO other plans. The future looked empty and foreboding.

Exodus 33:14 (NKJV)

*"My presence will go with you,
and I will give you rest."*

In Monrovia, we had a memorial service for Tommy. Our friends from ELWA (the Drapers, the Reeds, and the de la Hayes) helped me plan Tommy's funeral service. Ray and Sophie were so encouraging to me. Sophie, also a writer, had given me several little books to read: Thomas à Kempis' The Imitation of Christ; The Loveliness of Christ taken from the letters of Samuel Rutherford; The Greatest Thing in the World, by Henry Drummond, and Comforted of God, by Bridget O'Brien. She had marked passages and pages for me that she thought would be especially helpful in the days and weeks ahead. Over the years I have been refreshed many times by the words in those little books written so long ago and so lovingly given to me in my hour of desperate need.

"A Time for War"

During all the sadness and sorrow unfolding around me, there was yet another 'wrinkle' affecting my plans for leaving Liberia.

Civil unrest which had heated up down in South Africa had reached the boiling point. All major airlines were filled to capacity with non- African foreigners (mostly white) fleeing for their lives. Many of them left in such a hurry that they left with only the clothes on their backs. The problems had to do with the Sharpsville atrocities and massacres happening in South Africa. But what did all of that have to do with my leaving West Africa? It was because of that unrest there was not a single, available seat on any airline out of Monrovia! Those planes flying into Monrovia came from South Africa and were already filled to capacity; no one deplaned there. It would remain that way for at least another seven weeks, I was told!

But God is faithful! Some friends of ours were missionaries who lived in Greenville, just 15 minutes flying time from Tournata. They were affectionately known as Pa and Ma Wallen. They were both in their 60s and still doing amazing things in the Lord's work. Pa Wallen had even taught himself how to fly. When Pa Wallen would fly and before every one of his take-offs, he prayed. He also prayed before he landed his plane. Many times we would hear Pa Wallen "buzz" the Tournata airstrip in his old Aeronca Champ airplane. Tommy had commented to me once, "You have to try really hard to crash an Aeronca Champ airplane! It's one of the safest airplanes Pa Wallen could fly." Pa Wallen amazed us with his dependence on God alone to get him safely wherever he needed to go! You might remember the Second Corinthians Scripture that says, "We walk by faith, not by sight." Pa Wallen flew by faith! All those who knew him knew that to be true and we admired his trust in God alone for his safety.

The Wallens had not been home to Canada on furlough for six or seven years. They were in Monrovia, packed and ready to take their flight when they learned of Tommy's death. They insisted that we use their airline tickets, thus making it possible for the three of us to fly home to

Texas. Their act of love, though, required them to return to Greenville, unpack their belongings and stay there for another six or seven weeks. It would take that amount of time before they could procure passage again to leave Liberia. The love shown by my brother and sister in Christ in this way made my most difficult situation much easier to bear.

"A Time to Embrace"

A few days after Tommy's Liberian funeral, I received a message from Walt Knowles asking me if I would fly to Tournata one last time to say goodbye. I thought by that time I had cried all the tears I could, but I was wrong! Datco flew me to Tournata. We didn't stay long there, maybe half an hour. All of our African friends and our missionary friends had gathered together by the airstrip for our final farewell. While holding hands they sang to me, "God Be with You till We Meet Again." I knew that I'd never see my precious friends again this side of heaven. It was such an emotional moment for me and for all of us. It was almost more than I could bear. My heart was broken having to leave my faithful friends who were from all over the world. But Christians do have that blessed hope of seeing one another again in heaven.

A young African, Samuel (Sammy) K. Solo, my former houseboy who had been standing by the plane, approached me with a little white envelope. "Ma," he said, "this is for you. We want you to have it." I hugged him, along with the other African men and their wives; then I boarded the plane to return to Monrovia. It was not until we were in the air flying back to Monrovia that I opened the lumpy and bulging envelope. On a piece of ruled paper and written in pencil was a list of about 10 names. That list reflected names of young African men we had known and loved during our time at Tournata. But the envelope also had money in it. Some of the men had given an amount equaling a week's salary or more. I was so deeply touched by their love and generosity. Their act of love reminded me of Paul's writing about the Macedonian church when he said of them:

2 Corinthians 8:2 (Amplified Version)

"...in the midst of an ordeal of severe tribulation, their abundance of joy and their depth of poverty (together) have overflowed in a wealth of lavish generosity on their part."

That gift for my children and me has been one of the most precious gifts I've EVER received. It was given in love; it was given sacrificially. I was deeply humbled.

"A Time to Keep"

Sadly, the day arrived for the children and me to leave Liberia. Upon our arrival at Robert's Field, about an hour's drive from Monrovia, there were already a huge number of people there. I was overwhelmed. I hadn't thought that people would drive so far, but they did. All of our Datco friends, our missionary friends, and Tommy's business acquaintances were there. All of them had made their way to Robert's Field to say goodbye to me. I was deluged with emotions as their presence saddened, encouraged and blessed me all at the same time. I had only one goal for that moment and it was to live through my departure from Liberia. My heart was broken, having to leave all of them. They had been such a part of my life in Liberia, the only life I'd known for the past three years of marriage.

It had been Datco's custom to present each pilot's wife a special gift on her birthday. My October birthday was still six months away but Charlotte, my dear friend and upstairs neighbor, came to me just as I was boarding the plane. She said to me, "Ginger, I want you take this. I can get another one here." In my hand she placed a beautiful American ten-dollar-gold-piece necklace. I began to cry so hard that I wasn't able to see to board the plane. I was so touched by her desire to give me something that she valued so much. Throughout the years, I have treasured Charlotte's gift to me. When I remember our parting, even to this day, it brings tears to my eyes. Love is like that; it is both bitter and sweet.

"A Time to be Silent"

Six weeks after leaving Robert's Field and after Tommy's body arrived by ship, there was another funeral for Tommy; this time in Houston, Texas. Our friends and relatives needed to have their own opportunity to say their goodbyes to Tommy. This was not how Tommy and I had envisioned coming home to Houston.

Once again, my wounds of grief were ripped open and fresh grief consumed me. Some, I learned later, had thought my quiet, solemn attitude was not grief. I was criticized for not shedding more tears at his Houston funeral. But I had already grieved greatly at Tommy's Liberian funeral. In addition, my grief was both personal and private. Allowing myself to cry openly among so many people or in my children's presence was not an option for me. My two-year-old Vicki was especially sensitive to my tears and I knew that I must be strong for her. Grief, I've learned, is an individual thing. However, one chooses to grieve, others need to allow him/her that privilege. No two people grieve in the same way or for the same length of time. But God is faithful and He used my very young children to help keep me focused on their needs instead of the all-consuming sorrow locked in my heart.

"A Time to Speak"

Through Tommy's death, God has taught me many things about Himself. I'm sure that I wouldn't have learned them in any other way. I've listed only eight of them to illustrate some of what God allowed me to understand, but there was so much more.

Life is way too short; don't waste it. We have nothing but today; live it for Him!

Don't depend on others for your relationship with God. Through Tommy's death, God drew me to Himself. Don't wait for tragedy to strike; turn to Him NOW.

Following the death of a loved one, disregard the ignorant and even hurtful things some people may say to you. Most of them mean well. They may not know how to express their own sorrow for you or for your situation. And that's okay. Forgive them if they say it wrong.

God is trustworthy. God is faithful. God is fair. BELIEVE it! It is true!

Stay in the Word and learn of Him; you can't have a relationship with someone you don't know!

Never doubt God's love for you. He willingly gave His own Son to die for your sin and mine. That is real love.

Get involved in your church, your community or some ministry that will keep your mind occupied with good things while you heal.

Lastly, give yourself permission to grieve; it is a healthy thing. It is the only way you can heal emotionally.

Ecclesiastes 3:11

"He has made everything appropriate in its time."

PART 2—LIFE BACK IN THE STATES

After Tommy's second funeral service, I tried very hard to pick up the pieces of my life for Randy and Vicki's sake. We did all of the usual things, such as going to church, grocery shopping and visiting family and friends. But life for the three of us was difficult without Tommy. I was okay until Vicki would ask, "When is Daddy coming home?" I would sit down with her and explain to her, "Don't you remember? Daddy's in heaven with Jesus now and he isn't going to be able to come back." Vicki repeated that scene every two or three days. She kept forgetting and I found it necessary to tell her again and again. It hurt me to see her in so much pain. She tried to sort through everything to understand about death and dying. I didn't expect her to be able to comprehend; I found it too difficult for even me to grasp.

It was during that time my sister Barbara called me from California. She, her husband George and their three children had not been able to attend Tommy's funeral in Texas. But Barbara had called me to say, "One day you will need to get away for a time. And when you do, come visit us here in Long Beach." Barbara was correct.

A few weeks later during Vacation Bible School, I dropped by the nursery to check on Randy. The lady in charge of the nursery was the mom of my close friend Barbara Ann from high school. She said to me, "Why don't you call Barbara Ann? My brother in Hawaii has wanted her to come there to visit him and his family.

On your return, you could visit your sister Barbara in California." That is what I did.

Four weeks later, on our return from Hawaii, Barbara Ann and I visited my sister and her family in Long Beach. We had a great time. But when it was time for Barbara Ann to return to Houston, I wasn't ready to leave. Barbara Ann had to return to her job. Since there had been so little time to spend with my sister, I delayed leaving. After a couple of weeks, Barbara said to me, "Ginger, why don't you fly Mom and Dad here with your children? Then all of us could enjoy visiting together." She continued, "Maybe you need a little more time here with us. Having Vicki and Randy here with you would allow you to stay as long as you want."

That is how I became a California resident.

CHAPTER 8
Falling Head Over Heels

Vicki Lynn, Ginger and Randy

One day while my brother-in-law George was at work, Barbara and I searched for apartments close to each other. I had decided to stay in Long Beach to try and make a home for Randy, Vicki and me. Barbara and I began our search for just the right place for us. Finally, we found and rented two apartments, side by side. Days later, Barbara and I moved her family of five into one apartment; I moved into the other one. George left for work one day from their lovely, rented Spanish-style home and came home to a much smaller apartment. I don't think he ever forgave me for that, but it was wonderful having family next door to us. It was a sacrifice for them to do that, but it was a very big blessing for my children and me.

It wasn't a large apartment complex where we moved; it was only 10 units. But it was small enough to quickly learn about "the bachelors;" they lived in the bottom corner apartment. I had met one of them, Dick Hovis. The bachelors worked different hours and rarely were the four of them home at the same time. Dick, though, was soon to be married. On occasion, I would talk with Dick while I hung clothes (diapers) on the lines next to his parking space. Two of the other guys I'd seen, but had never met them. And the fourth bachelor I had not seen or met.

I had a corner apartment. Randy and Vicki's bedroom was located on the side of the building next to the covered parking area. Very early every morning I could hear the kids giggling and laughing. But by the time I got to their room, all that I could see was both of them sitting and giggling on Randy's bed. Early one morning, I heard both children giggling again. I tiptoed quietly to their room. I saw Vicki helping Randy chin himself up to the window. And they were both waving to someone. I peeked out the curtain and saw a very nice-looking man waving back at them. I learned later that the "waver" was bachelor number four, named Les.

One particular trip to the beauty salon was anything but what I had expected. I had decided, on the spur of the moment, to get my haircut. I had kept my hair long and usually wore it in a ponytail for convenience. But that day I had decided to have it cut. I made two major mistakes that day: 1) I was not paying attention to what the beautician was doing, and 2) I wasn't facing the mirror. The young beautician must have gotten carried away. When she turned the chair around and I looked in the mirror, I could hardly believe my eyes! I looked like Peter Pan. It was an EXTREMELY short haircut! I cried! There was NOTHING else to do but cry! I morosely left the beauty salon for home and as quickly as possible. When I knocked on Barbara's door, she looked at me and said, "Well, it's cute. But if you don't like it, it will all grow out again!" I cried again.

Later as I carried my garbage to the dumpster, I rounded a corner and ran right into the "waver" guy. After he pushed himself away from me, still trying to hold me upright, his first words were, "What in the world happened to your hair?" That was not a great introduction and most certainly not conducive to a budding friendship. I slowly backed away from him and excused myself, hurrying to empty my garbage. On my way back to my apartment, I stopped by Barbara's and said, "I just met this GUY and he wanted to know what happened to my hair!" Then I cried again. I thought that if a total stranger had noticed my hair, I must look REALLY terrible!

Because Barbara and George's family of three children was increasing, they decided to look for a home to buy. They had no problem locating one and they moved within a few weeks. The day after they moved, there was a knock at my door. I opened the door and there stood Les, the hair critic/waver guy. He asked me, "Would you like to go out tonight to dinner with me; then maybe see a movie afterwards?"

I was dumbfounded AND I was still a little miffed over Les' comment about my hair. But I think that I startled him when I said, "I don't know. I need to think about it." "When do think you might know?" he persisted. "Give me a couple of hours," I replied. Two hours later there was another knock at my door. I opened the door. There he stood, leaning against the doorjamb. Before he could ask, I said to him, "Alright, I'll go to dinner and to a movie with you."

I called a baby-sitter for the kids and got myself ready for our date. "The Manhattan Restaurant," a very upscale restaurant in Long Beach, was the place he chose to take me. It was elegant, classy and the food was exquisite. Les, dressed in a gorgeous, gray pinstriped suit, looked quite handsome. Our conversation flowed easily on a variety of subjects and mutual interests. I thought to myself, "Great eating place, terrific food, wonderful conversation with a handsome guy; what more could I want?" I'm not sure what I expected. But after our rocky beginning, the evening was going exceptionally well thus far. He was polite, thoughtful, courteous and attentive. I thought to myself, "This was a good beginning to an evening that almost didn't happen."

Then it was time to see the movie, The Misfits, with Clark Gable and Marilyn Monroe. There was a line of people that wound around the theater waiting to buy tickets. The reason? Clark Gable had unexpectedly died of a heart attack in the final shooting days of the movie. Everyone wanted to see his final movie. The theater was packed. We were escorted to the balcony and that was okay. But after the movie ended, we walked toward the stairs. I had on a pair of new, patent leather heels, which were shiny and slick on the soles. With the theater being packed, someone pushed me from behind and I went careening down the stairs. Les was trying to catch me. I was totally humiliated by my fall! After he helped me up, through clenched teeth I said to Les, "Take me home!" He was trying to ask me if I was okay, but once again I said, "Just take me home!" I wanted to evaporate or disappear from the face of the earth! I was too embarrassed to EVER see this man again!

The drive home was in total humiliated silence. He walked me to my apartment and I opened my door. I was about to shut it firmly and forever when he stopped me and said, "If you're willing to risk going out with me again, I'm willing to risk it, too." For some reason (maybe hysteria?), his comment made me laugh. Had he not said that, I would NEVER have seen him again! Humiliation and embarrassment had overwhelmed me, but Les defused the whole situation with his humorous comment. The two of us have laughed many times about my "falling" for him on our first date.

While I was dating Les, I was also dating other guys. Flowers, roses in particular, were being delivered to my apartment frequently. It seemed my life was like an old Lucille Ball movie. I was running back and forth making sure that the flowers on display matched the guy coming to the door. I kept roses in the bathtub behind the shower curtain because I had run out of places to put them.

A couple of the guys I had met at church, one in particular, had become rather important to me. But dating with children became the acid test in those relationships. Children have a way of exposing character traits, especially negative ones that might otherwise have taken years to expose. Not many single guys can handle a kid who just threw up on him. And it became clear to me what life would be like living with a person who couldn't adapt to children and their unexpected illnesses.

One by one the list of guys was narrowed down to just Les. One evening the four of us sat on the floor around my coffee table; we were eating Chinese food with chopsticks. Vicki, my three- year old, whispered loudly to me, "Mommy, why doesn't Mr. Les just be our daddy and stay here with us?"

I was paralyzed by her question! Even worse, I knew Les had heard her because he was grinning like a Cheshire cat. I remember saying to her, "But Honey, Mr. Les is our friend and he can't stay with us."

She quickly responded, "Oh, but we have room! He can sleep in your big bed with you."

I choked on my egg roll and said to her, "No, he can't! He has to go home!" But THAT was the type of situation in which I found myself while dating with young children! Kids do say the doggonedest things!

There were many endearing things about Les. One in particular was how he planned our times together. He would plan the entire day and he included the children. A couple of times we drove to San Diego for a day at the zoo and then returned to Long Beach. Often we would change clothes and go out again for the evening. Some of the time the kids were part of the evening plans as well. But at other times, Les hired a sitter so that just the two of us could go out together. One of the best things about dating Les was that I never really knew what to expect. He was amazingly creative in finding interesting and unusual things for all of us to do together. Les seemed to sense the times when I needed space.

Being a single parent and on duty 24/7 was difficult at times. But it was his sensitivity to me and to my needs that made Les one very special man. He courted me in a way that gained my respect and admiration for him. We dated for three months before he ever kissed me. Afterwards, I said to him, "What took you so long?"

Smiling, he admitted to me, "I didn't want to rush you and I didn't want to make a mistake by doing something wrong. I couldn't risk losing you. I could wait until the time was right!" And he did.

We dated for about eight months and we broke up twice during that time; both times it was my decision. I would ask him about his relationship with Christ. Because his answers didn't match my Baptist vernacular, I thought he wasn't a Christian. But after some very long talks, I was able to see that Les was authentic in his relationship with Christ. Once I was assured of that, then we could progress in our relationship. Establishing that fact was pivotal for me.

On May 27, 1961, Les and I were married. He was 28 years old and I was 21. Our lives were almost idyllic. That same year we purchased our first home. We couldn't have been happier.

Ginger and Les married one week

Four years later, Les, the kids and I moved to Texas. We had received a phone call from my mom saying that my dad's doctor had given him a short time to live. I went to Les and asked him to give us time with my dad. That would allow the kids to get to know both of their grandparents. I told him if he would do that, I would go any place in the world with him afterwards. He agreed and we moved to Texas later that same year. Once again, Les did something that most guys wouldn't have done. He gave up his budding career in California and moved to Texas without a job waiting for him. But as he has said, "Career-wise, it was the smartest move I've ever made." The oil industry was at its peak in the '60s and Les was able to plug into that industry in Houston. Les' career was going well and life was good for us.

We had chosen to live north of Houston in Conroe, a town known as "the bedroom of Houston." Both of our kids were involved in school activities that kept them and me busy. Les' commute to work was three hours, round-trip, five days a week. But the decision we had made was worth the sacrifices. We knew where our children were and who their friends were. For Les and me, that was important to us.

Psalm 31:15 (NIV)

"My times are in Your hands..."

CHAPTER 9
The Road to Ethiopia

When a friend telephoned Les on a Sunday afternoon, I never could have known how that one telephone call would change our lives forever. The caller was our friend Robert Rountree. He and his wife Monyeen had a Bible study in their home that Les and I, along with others, attended. The year was 1971 and we were living in Conroe, Texas. The reason Robert called was to ask Les if he would attend a Sunday evening service at First Baptist Church (FBC). The speaker was to be a missionary doctor from Ethiopia. The doctor had a slide presentation of his work up in the Menz (munz) area of Ethiopia, almost 12,000 feet in elevation. We learned that evening that Menz was the same village where Haile Selassie, the former Emperor of Ethiopia, was born.

After Robert's phone call, Les and I met Robert and Monyeen at church that night. We listened as Dr. Sam Cannata spoke and showed slides of his work. Because I had lived in Africa and lived on the mission field back in the late '50s and early '60s, I was very interested in Dr. Cannata's work. I loved Africa! But I knew that Les was not particularly interested in missions or in becoming a missionary. I had not pressed the issue concerning missions in spite of my previous involvement, but I did pray about it. With the faithful prayers of five of my very special friends, this was a concern on my heart that just wouldn't go away. But that Sunday evening's service was especially wonderful. During Dr. Cannata's presentation, he made a comment that had escaped my attention. But Les heard it and remembered it. At the conclusion of Dr.

Cannata's slide show, due to the press of the crowd, neither Les nor I was able to meet with him. But what Dr. Cannata had said, Les stored away in his heart.

Only a couple of weeks later Les and I were eating in a Chinese restaurant in Houston. Les leaned across the table and said to me, "You know what I want to do?" I said, "No. What do you want to do?" He said quite calmly, "I'd like to go to Ethiopia to see Dr. Cannata." I stared at him for a second. Then I said, "You wouldn't go!" and I kept eating my egg roll. Then he said to me, "Yes, I would." After about the third time that he repeated those words, I began to wonder if he really would go. I couldn't understand at the time why Les would want to travel to Ethiopia to see a missionary doctor; that puzzled me! After all, Ethiopia was not a country located just around the corner. It was a long way from Houston, Texas; indeed, it was better than halfway around the world. I reasoned that Les wasn't even attending church regularly! I must admit that I was stunned by his desire to travel so far to see a man he had never met. The whole thing seemed oddly interesting to me.

I decided as we sat in that Chinese restaurant to put Les to the test. KLM (Royal Dutch Airlines) was my favorite overseas airline to fly. Its office was just down the street from the restaurant. I said to Les, "Okay, let's just go there and check out ticket prices." After our query with KLM, we were amazed to learn that it was several thousand dollars and WAY out of our price range. Both Les and I were more than a little disappointed. I think we were that day what the Bible called "downcast." But later that day I called Dr. Cannata. He was staying with family members for a few more days in the Houston area. Over the phone, I introduced myself to Dr. Cannata and told him all about Les' desire to visit him in Ethiopia. He was very pleased, but he told me that we needed to wait until after the rainy season was over. Dry season, the best time to visit, would not occur again until the following September. I knew that a lot could happen in almost a year's time.

After leaving the KLM office and talking with Dr. Cannata, Les and I continued our talks about the trip to Ethiopia. But due to the outlandish travel fees, it seemed impossible for us to go. I continued to pray about it and I asked my praying friends to pray also. One of those friends was Ava Hellard, who owned the Christian Bookstore in Conroe. Every Monday morning in Ava's bookstore, six of us met for prayer. Faithfully the group prayed for many things, but our focus was on a strong Bible-teaching church, godly husbands and our children. Members of that group included Ava Hellard, Dorothy Nichols, Madonna Marley, Pat Carter and a black lady named Ruby Anderson, plus myself. Ruby couldn't meet with us as often as she wanted because she lived in a small neighboring community. But we met for two years and saw God's answers to many of our prayers. Our group experienced true "koinonia" fellowship. Koinonia is a

Greek word that means loving fellowship with God and within the body of Christ. Whatever one needed, the rest of us tried to meet that need. It was a beautiful thing to see and experience. And it is the very thing God desires for all of the body of Christ.

Several times after Dr. Cannata's visit to FBC, I would attend the prayer time with my bookstore friends. I would say to them, "Pray! Things at Les' work are making him doubt our being able to make this trip. He has told me that he cannot be gone at that particular time." The group would pray diligently about the situation all week. The following week when we met together, I said to them, "Les came in from work and said that the work problem had been resolved. It looked like we could go after all." That same scenario would repeat itself five or six times before our Ethiopian trip.

Still, there remained the excessive costs of our plane fare to Ethiopia; we needed cheaper flights. One day I happened to be in the offices of FBC sharing with my friend Dolores Lewis; she was one of the FBC's secretaries. She mentioned a travel agency for Christians in Florida. She gave me the name and address of the organization and immediately I wrote to them. I inquired about the same itinerary that I had given to KLM. The itinerary included places I loved to visit: Amsterdam, Lisbon, Athens and Rome.

We could visit those places on our way to and from Ethiopia. With my letter in hand, I sat outside on the curb by our mailbox and prayed before mailing my "wish list" to the travel agency. I remember saying to God, "This trip was not my idea. I think that it was something YOU have laid on Les' heart. But God, You know that we need affordable tickets." I finished praying, got up and mailed the letter.

I waited rather impatiently for a reply to my letter. Two weeks passed before I received the travel agency's answer. Once again I sat down on the curb by our mailbox and prayed before opening the letter. I reminded the Lord of what we could afford (as if HE didn't know already). I remember mentioning to Him that if necessary, He could change the amount of the ticket price if it was too high. Then I thanked Him for whatever was written in the letter and opened it. The total ticket price was only $1,300.00 for BOTH of us, ROUND trip! I hurried home so that I could fall on my knees in privacy to praise God. What an awesome Father our God is!

Isaiah 41:13

"For I am the Lord your God, who upholds your right hand, Who says to you, 'Do not fear, I will help you."

Because of our children's involvement in school and other activities, they did not want to go with Les and me to Ethiopia. My mother came to stay with them in our home so that they could carry on with their regular routine. Vicki was 14 years old and Randy was 12. At that time they were not interested in traveling overseas with us. We were grateful to see God's provision for their care via my mom. She came to stay with them during our 19-day trip.

Our Ethiopian trip was made that September after the rainy season just as Dr. Cannata had instructed us. That trip was the result of a year of many answered prayers.

Back in 1960 I had left Africa when my first husband Tommy, a pilot, was killed in a plane crash. Tommy and I had served with

Tournata, R. G. LeTourneau's mission in Liberia, West Africa. When I returned to the States (and before Les and I were married),

I had financially supported Missionary Aviation Fellowship's (MAF) organization. There were two couples, Ray and Carolyn Morgret and Carol and Tom Albright, who served with MAF. Ray, Carolyn and Carol had served at Tournata with Tommy and me back in the late '50s and early '60s. After Les and I were married, we had continued to be a part of their ministries, financially and prayerfully.

When Les and I arrived in Addis Ababa, Ethiopia, we discovered that we needed to fly to the Menz area where Dr. Sam (as he became fondly known) and Ginny lived. The only other option was a 12- hour drive by Land Rover over rutted, dirt roads. We chose to fly MAF. For Les and me, it was the "icing on the cake." Flying with MAF allowed us to see and experience first-hand the results of our years of contributions to that organization. An MAF airplane was used to fly us to Dr. Sam and Ginny's home. The airstrip in Menz had only been completed the day before our arrival. The pilot, Les and I landed on that tiny Menz strip in the little MAF single-engine plane. The pilot flew over the newly constructed airstrip a couple of times to make sure it was in good landing condition. The Cannata's daughter Kathy stood atop their Land Rover and held up a roll of toilet paper streaming in the wind. She was our living windsock for our landing. A slight drizzle fell at the 14,000-foot elevation; the pilot told us that it was clouds, not rain. After more than a year of prayer and planning, we had finally arrived safely. We were totally exhausted and were experiencing some effects of the high altitude.

Many things impressed me about Ethiopia. Some Ethiopians appeared almost European with their delicate facial features. Their finely chiseled features and wavy hair were nothing like those of the Liberians. Ethiopian people also had lighter skin tones. In addition, their body type was smaller with slimmer frames.

But the wind velocity really caught us by surprise. In addition, the wind blew all the time. People wore coverings over their faces and heads because of the wind. I had lived in the lowlands of Liberia where it was hot and humid. But up in Menz, it was very cold. Dr. Sam and Ginny had a nice home (by missionary standards) with a fireplace. Now, I could see the need for heat, especially early in the mornings.

On the first day after we arrived, Ginny's wringer-type washing machine was torn down to the last nut and bolt. The parts were spread out on a tarpaulin in a small laundry room outside the house. From the appearance of the scattered parts, I would not have guessed that it was a washing machine; it appeared to be a pile of junk! But with Les' mechanical mind at work, that pile of junk soon became a washing machine again. It was in working order that same afternoon. And I was very impressed with my guy!

Almost immediately after our arrival, Les had begun to be sick. Severe headaches began to plague him. Everyday Dr. Sam would have to give Les injections for the pain, dizziness and nausea. He spent a portion of each day lying down and resting with symptoms of severe altitude sickness. Yet he continued to help Dr. Sam in many ways the entire time we were there. Looking back at our continual struggles to even make the trip, it became obvious that our problems had been the result of spiritual warfare. Dr. Sam's clinic was only about a hundred feet from his home. One evening Dr. Sam and Les walked over to the clinic and found a man waiting there who had been speared in the side. Dr. Sam came and asked me if I'd like to assist him in surgery. "Of course," I answered. However, I knew NOTHING about assisting in surgery. Dr. Sam said to me, "Just listen to what I'm about to tell you." Then he told me what he planned to do in surgery. He named the instruments he would be using and laid them out on a table.

The little, old man walked into surgery with his dirty blanket wrapped around him and crawled up on the operating table. Dr. Sam took his hand in his and prayed for him in Amharic, the national language of Ethiopia. Then he gave him an injection of Ketalar, an intravenous general anesthetic. Almost instantly the old man went to sleep. Dr. Sam began surgery to repair the colon; he performed a temporary colostomy. Les and Dr. Sam had devised a colostomy bag from a Zip-lock bag and duct tape! The surgery went well, but I became nervous when Dr. Sam asked the man some questions in Amharic and the man responded. I said to Dr. Sam, "Look, give him some more Ketalar! It'll make ME feel better." Dr. Sam told me that the man wasn't feeling any pain, BUT he did give him a bit more Ketalar. After suturing him, the man woke up. He got up from the operating table with his dirty blanket still wrapped around him and walked to one of the cots in the clinic. There he lay down and stayed the night. He left the next morning promising to return in a week, which he did. Once again, Dr. Sam repeated the surgical procedure.

However, this time he reversed the colostomy. The man was able to go home the following day. Not once did the man have an infection or ANY other complication. I was amazed by the things Dr. Sam was able to do with so few amenities.

In the evening we gathered together for our usual devotional time. But Les was so ill that most nights Dr. Sam had to give him something to make him sleep. One particular night I sat on the edge of our bed holding Les' hand. He said to me, "I'm sorry, Honey, that I'm not the religious person that you want me to be." His statement stunned me! I loved Les with all my heart and prayed for him daily. I had never said a word to him or had given him any reason to say those words to me! But what he'd said to me confirmed in my heart two things: the first was that this trip was all about what God was doing in Les' heart; the second was that the headaches and general malaise that Les was experiencing were indeed indications of spiritual warfare. Back in the States, Les had been a very active and healthy person. But since our arrival in Menz, Les was ill most of the time. I shared my thoughts about spiritual warfare with Dr. Sam and Ginny. We began to ask God for His protection and in particular to help us in this area.

Our visit with Dr. Sam and Ginny came to an end much too soon. Now it was time for us to leave. The effects that our trip to Ethiopia had on us were truly amazing. However, not all were apparent at the time. In fact, it took almost 10 years for us to see the profound effects that the answers to our prayers had.

And that was when Les and I were accepted to serve with Wycliffe Bible Translators as missionaries. After 18 months of training, we were sent to the Philippine Islands to begin our own missionary journey. Many times I've wondered, "What if I'd given up praying for Les and for his spiritual walk with the Lord? And what if I'd not taken Les seriously when he said that he wanted to go to Ethiopia?" I pondered those things in my heart as I reflected on God's character. God knew Les' heart and mine as well. As a result of what God did in our lives through prayer, I've often wondered how many wives have given up too soon in praying for their husbands. Or how many husbands have given up believing that they would ever see a difference in their wives or in their relationships with Christ?

Satan is such a deceiver! Indeed, he is the "Father of Lies" as the Scripture says. He is constantly deceiving us. Discouragement is his special tool that he uses to keep us focused on the negative traits of our mates. We must NOT allow him to do that. Since Satan is the accuser, he will bring up your past or your mate's past to keep you from trusting God. But our prayers and our praises to God will cause him to flee! Satan can't stand to hear God's children pray to Him. When you think that you are experiencing a spiritual battle, begin to praise God for His victory in your life and the Enemy will flee.

James 4:7

*"Submit therefore to God.
Resist the devil and he will flee from you."*

CHAPTER 10
Taking Spanish and Other Lessons

I'm not a linguist. In Jr. High School, I took Latin because I had thought about becoming an attorney. I wasn't good at Latin and I barely squeaked by. But having to choose between Latin and Spanish, I chose Latin. Looking back at my earlier years in school, I made two critical blunders when I chose which classes to take. The first one was NOT choosing to take Spanish; the second was in NOT taking typing.

I had lived in Africa. But, of course, there Latin had been no help to me at all. Even when I traveled to Africa through Portugal, it did not help me to decipher which room was the ladies' restroom! I had been taught that Latin was the root of ALL languages. How I had been misled! While in Portugal, it was necessary for me to wait for a lady to go into the restroom so that I could know which was the right one for me. I've said all of this for you to see the importance of language training and in as many languages as possible. One can never know whether God's future plans might involve some far-off land. There He can show us that even some of our blunders begin to make sense. That is the way it happened for me.

Les and I were living in Conroe, Texas. By this time our two children were grown and living away from home. Randy was 21, single and owned his own home. Our 23-year-old Vicki was married to David Hellard, son of Ava Hellard mentioned in The Road to Ethiopia; the year was 1980.

Because I am an avid reader, I had a favorite bookstore I frequented. One day as I started into the bookstore, I noticed a sign placed on the inside of the glass door just at eye level; I could not miss seeing it! The sign read:

"WANT TO LEARN CONVERSATIONAL SPANISH? LEARN FROM A 'NATIONAL.' CALL ALICIA…"

Her phone number was on the sign and I reached into my purse for a pen and paper to jot down the number. I called Alicia when I got home and set up a time to talk with her about lessons for my husband and me. Our meeting went well and Les and I began to meet with Alicia a couple of times a week. Eventually Les stopped taking lessons. His three-hour drive to work in Houston and back again, along with his fluctuating work hours, just didn't work out. Under those circumstances, language training for him was almost impossible. Afterwards, it was just Alicia and me. Our friendship blossomed and developed on a deeper level.

Les and I had begun to consider going into some sort of mission work overseas. We had sent inquiries to a host of mission organizations seeking to find where we felt God wanted us. Alicia was interested in our situation, but in a somewhat casual way. I continued lessons with her even though I still had no desire to be sent to a Spanish-speaking country. It was, as the King stated so aptly in the movie, *The King and I*, "a puzzlement" to me. But I persevered with my Spanish. Even though I was no linguist, I did learn some words and phrases. And who knows? Maybe they would come in handy someday. Just maybe. Alicia came from Guadalajara, Mexico. Her dad played with the Mexican Philharmonic Orchestra. She had siblings who were doctors, dentists, musicians and attorneys. She was a trained librarian. Alicia's husband was an American and Caucasian; they had a son Lalo about two years old. Alicia didn't know how to drive a car. Since her husband traveled all the time, Alicia was at home most of the time. I soon discovered that, in a small way, I was her link to the outside world because I spent time with her.

The lessons continued until Les and I were accepted as members of WBT. When we became members of that organization, it was necessary for Les to give up his job, sell our home and move to Dallas for an 18-month, management training course. Once we had accomplished all of those things, we were invited to join the Philippine Branch of WBT as support missionaries. In August 1984, we left for Manila, Philippines.

One of the things WBT wanted for all its members was to learn the language. Though several dominant languages are present in the Philippines, then-President Ferdinand Marcos declared Tagalog to be the official language. After our four-month training time with the national translation organization, both Les and I went to language school. The surprise for us was learning that within the Tagalog language there were 1,500 pure Spanish words. For over 100 years, the Spaniards controlled the Philippine Islands, all 7,107 of them. But in a small section of the city in

Manila, near the American Embassy, to this day they speak pure Castilian Spanish. My point in this history lesson is that my Spanish lessons were not in vain. During my lifetime I have discovered that, when God places a "yen" in my heart to do or to learn something, it is ALWAYS for a good reason. You can be sure it will not be wasted! Actually, I had a head start in my Tagalog training because of my Spanish lessons that I had taken from Alicia in Texas.

Jeremiah 29:11

"For I know the plans that I have for you," declares the Lord, "plans for welfare and not for calamity to give you a future and a hope."

Les and I stayed in the Philippines for two years before our first furlough to the States. While visiting our daughter Vicki and her husband in Conroe, I received an urgent phone call from Alicia. It surprised me that she knew we were back in the States since we'd only just arrived. She said that she HAD to see me. I asked Vicki if I could use her car to go and see Alicia; she handed me her keys. I was not sure what to expect as I punched her doorbell button. As soon as she opened the door, I knew that something was wrong. She invited me in and I sat down on her sofa. Alicia came to me and dropped to her knees at my feet. She said these words, "Whatever you have, I want!" I said to her, "Alicia, do you mean Jesus?" She simply responded, "Yes." And at that moment Alicia and I prayed together. She trusted Christ to be her Savior. We hugged and cried and talked for a while and then I left her. What an awesome experience to see Alicia born into the kingdom of God! Our furlough time had become even more precious to me. God had allowed me to see Alicia's new faith in Christ. It was better than I could have dreamed!

After my return to Vicki's house, I called my friend Gerrie Schaefer and asked her if she would be willing to do two things. She said, "Yes, what are they?" I asked her, "Would you be willing to teach Alicia to drive a car and would you lead her in a basic Bible study?" She agreed to do both of those things. With our limited time in the States and so many churches and people to see, God removed my concerns for Alicia's spiritual growth through Gerrie. Just being able to see the body of Christ function as He designed it is a beautiful thing. We are important to one another as we live to fulfill His plans.

Corinthians 12:12 (NIV)

"The body is a unit, though it is made up of many parts; and though all its parts are many, they form one body..."

Looking back, there are several seemingly unrelated events that began to fall into place. But it was necessary for God to give me His insight and wisdom in order to see them.

First, He had to give me the desire to take Spanish. At that time, there was no urgent reason why I should even consider taking Spanish. But God in His omniscience KNEW that Les and I would be assigned to the Philippine Islands with its Spanish history. And He knew that the

Tagalog language was filled with pure Spanish words. Another thing I learned was that a name on a sign in a bookstore was a person who needed Jesus in her life. Having Alicia trust Christ as her Savior during our furlough was the "icing on the cake" for me. All of these unrelated events were gifts to Les and me. But I have wondered many times how I had missed seeing them. Perhaps it was because they came in such obscure ways that were unnoticed by me. Daily I pray to see His "busyness" within my life. In a world that clamors for ALL of our attention, there must be a time to be quiet and still so that we are able to see Him at work around us. We need to turn off the TV, unplug the I-pods and get quiet before Him.

Job 26:14 (NIV)

"And these are but the outer fringe of His works; how faint the whisper we hear of Him."

Back when I worked with college-age kids, often we sang a chorus with the words: "Open my eyes, Lord, we want to see Jesus, to reach out and touch Him and say that we love Him." That is my prayer for you and me. Opening our eyes to see God at work in and around our lives takes practice, time and QUIET. He is waiting to reveal Himself to us. The key to getting to know Him is to take time and make time to spend with Him. When we do, He will reveal Himself to us.

Daniel 2:28 (NIV)

"But there is a God in Heaven who reveals mysteries."

CHAPTER 11
When God Changes Your Plans

The idea of going to jungle camp in Mexico was one that evoked fear and trepidation in the heart of many a missionary trainee. Les and I, along with our friends, Leslie and Gordon Christian, were trainees with Wycliffe Bible Translators (WBT). We had thought long and hard about what was absolutely necessary to pack for our trip to Uvalde, Texas. The trip was for a three-month required training course. We had heard that it would be grueling and exhausting. It would test our mettle as nothing any of us had ever experienced. Les had some training experience because he had served in the Navy's Air Sea Rescue program. He might do very well or at least be able to survive the training!

The four of us had long conversations about some of the training requirements. All of us fretted about it to some extent. Except for Les and Gordon, I wondered how we ladies would be able to do what was expected of us without "wimping out." Gordon was an experienced hunter and outdoorsman; it just might be for him a walk in the park.

All of the jungle camp trainees had to determine what would be on their required list of ten essential items. Those items must be included with the other necessities in their one suitcase. All of the trainees were given a sheet of instructions listing the items to pack; some of those were a concern for me. For instance, we were told to bring: a length of rope, a tarpaulin, a hunting knife, a compass, eating and water utensils, rain ponchos, umbrellas, bug spray, a needle and thread, etc. I had an inkling that I was out of my depth and we hadn't left Dallas yet. Also, we needed to take one outfit suitable for church. I was sure that meant something akin to a skirt and blouse and not my usual church fare!

One day while shopping at a Drug Emporium in Dallas, Leslie and I found some mascara called "Marathon." It was supposed to last through thick and thin. We had planned our own time test for that item! Jungle training seemed the appropriate and perfect place to test its durability! We tossed that item into our suitcases along with our bathing suits, towels, and flip-flops (to be worn to the showers). Shampoo, BAND-AIDS, tape, gauze and antiseptic were all a must as well. But the flashlight with EXTRA batteries, toothpaste, toothbrushes and battery-powered radios did seem to be among the most standard requirements for us. In my heightened sense of anticipation for what lay ahead for us, those things seemed to be more comforting to me.

Looking over the list and needing to leave my best clothes at home, I was wondering if I could do all that was required of me. I continued with my packing but at the last moment just before we closed the suitcase, I threw in a very lightweight sheet-blanket. I remembered at that time I almost laughed because it was August. We were in hot Texas and we were heading for even hotter Uvalde, Texas, only a stone's throw from the Mexican border. But I tossed the blanket (another story) into the suitcase and slammed it shut. We were told we must do a 20-mile hike! In preparation for THAT, I began running more than my usual two to three miles a day. I had thought that by beefing up my running program, I would be able to keep up with the others. My biggest concern, though, was the required one-mile swim down the river. And since I didn't know how to swim, I was terrified! I fretted over that part of the training more than any of the rest. In my mind the swim was a monumental thing God would need to help me get through. But there was one more "biggy" for me—the killing of a chicken! Oh, how I anguished over both the swim and the chicken-killing events!

They dominated almost my every waking thought regarding our jungle camp training.

After talking this over with my friend Judy Satterfield in Conroe, Texas, she jokingly said to me, "Have you considered having the chicken stand on a log or something similar?

You could blindfold it and put a noose around its neck. Maybe give the chicken its last cigarette and then after its last remarks (by the chicken, of course), push the chicken off the log." We howled in laughter over her solution to my chicken- killing problem. It certainly seemed kinder than cutting the chicken's throat, which was the usual protocol! Actually, I had considered the noose part! Still, I was not at peace about the entire chicken-killing thing.

Some people asked me, "What about your faith? Did you not believe that God would take care of you in regard to both the swim AND the chicken-killing requirements?" Absolutely! And that was the only reason I could maintain any sense of normalcy while waiting for our jungle camp session to begin. I knew that God had some lessons for me to learn in the trust areas. But I also knew that unless I was willing to put myself out there, I would not be able to see God's power, His authority or faithfulness in my life. I knew that Les and I would need to experience Him wherever we were sent to serve Him as missionaries!

2 Chronicles 16:9 (NIV)

"For the eyes of the Lord range throughout the earth to strengthen those whose hearts are fully committed to Him."

I know that you know God is good, but I need to declare it once again. Of all those things I had feared the most, not one of them ever came to pass for Les and me! And that reminds me of a quote by Mark Twain, "I am an old man and have known a great many troubles, but most of them have never happened."

How could it have happened that we escaped going to jungle camp? Here's the rest of the story! Les and I, along with Gordon and Leslie, were ready to leave for jungle camp in Uvalde. All of our suitcases were packed and we were ready to be shuttled down there by van. But just one week before the jungle camp session was to begin, our session was canceled due to lack of experienced field missionaries to teach us. NEVER before in the history of the WBT had jungle camp ever been canceled. And yet, that is exactly what happened to us. The sighs of relief by the four of us could be heard all the way to the Mexican border!

But our sense of euphoria was short-lived! The following day, Les and I received a phone call from the WBT Philippine Branch Director Dave Ohlson, our new boss. He had heard about the latest wrinkle in our plans. And that posed a major problem for the Philippine branch because they were in dire need of us as replacements. We were needed to fill positions for other missionaries who needed to go to their home countries on furlough. But Dave had a new question for Les and me, "Would you be willing to come to the Philippines and train with the national Bible translation trainees?"

Dave's question was something that we had never considered as an option for us. There would be no good friends (Gordon and Leslie Christian) to encourage us daily and help get us through the training times together. I think too that knowing Les and I would be the only non-Filipinos to train with the group of 12 trainees concerned both of us. And we would be the oldest in the group as well. Being older within our American culture would not make much difference to other trainees, but within the Asian culture it was significant. Most of the other trainees were fresh out of college or had just launched their careers before they decided to become Bible translators. When given the opportunity to train with the Philippine nationals, Les and I wanted to be a part of that trailblazing experience. It seemed only logical for us to train within our host country. The added blessing for us was training with other people who had the same vision for Bible translation that we had.

Our training with the Translation Association of the Philippines (TAP) trainees was enriching. But it was by far the most stretching, the most faith-building, and the most educational experience that Les and I had ever encountered. Also, it involved the most significant time of spiritual growth that either of us had ever known. I had remembered reading in the Old Testament about Abraham where it said, "And Abraham walked with God" (as did Enoch, too). And in another place God said to Abraham, "Walk before Me." That was exactly what Les and I desired of God for us in our new training time with the national group. We wanted HIM to walk with us and to go before us. Only then would we be able to endure that severe time of testing and training.

1 Corinthians 10:13 (NIV)

"No temptation has overtaken you except such as is common to man, but God is faithful, who will not allow you to be tempted beyond what you are able, but with the temptation will also make the way of escape, that you may be able to bear it."

God is faithful and He was true to His Word in every way possible. But His ways surprised, blessed AND delighted us.

Part 3—Introduction to Life in Ilap

The TAP Trainees, August 1984

Our Field Training Course (FTC) group was an interesting mix of people that had congregated together. All of us had been led by the Lord to abandon careers, homes, families and future plans to follow God's plans. And yet we were all excited about that new chapter in our lives.

Janet Noblejas (no BLAY hahs) had worked for Kentucky Fried Chicken. She had been in an upper management position back in Manila. Monie Chiong had come from Cebu (say BOO), which was south of Luzon Island. His father was a sea captain there. But Monie had been with Navigators, a Christian organization working on college campuses all over the world. Jose and Anita Coronas were newly married; he was a pastor. Perla and Elgin were both nurses. The other trainees came from assorted, but interesting, backgrounds. I remember being so impressed by their strong faith in the Lord and their disciplined lives in their desire to follow Him. Those highly educated men and women were well on their way to becoming financially successful when God began to speak to each of their hearts.

Altogether there were a dozen trainees. We met together in Bagabag (bah GAH bug) for five days of orientation before being sent to an area on the big island of Luzon (loo SAHN) called Ifugao (EE fu gow). That particular area was chosen for our training for several reasons: the languages were more complex, isolation from people, and ruggedness of the terrain. Our training's purpose was to prepare us for being placed in new areas and in new language projects. The training's emphasis was to teach literacy, learn the language and ultimately to translate the New Testament. Not knowing the language, the culture, the available foods and the tribal people, many translation/literacy teams often experience undue stress and pressures. Our training was to teach us by experience what we could expect and how to cope with many of the daily challenges. We would be living in a village called Ilap (EE lop) which when translated meant "top of the mountain."

Our group was paired in teams of two, except for Perla, Tita and Elgin. Those three gals lived together in a nipa hut down the valley and across the mountain from Les and me. Early in the training session, Jose (Joe) and Anita Corona were forced to leave the training program. Joe became very ill with typhoid fever. Somewhere along the way he drank some contaminated water; that was a real "no-no." Up until that time they had been our closest trainee neighbors. They lived only down the mountain about 20 minutes from us. After Joe's illness, Monie Chiong and Eldon Talamisan (tal a MEE son) became our closest trainee neighbors. Their village was at the bottom of our mountain near the river. Eldon and Monie often stopped by our place as they hiked en route to other destinations. We always offered them Kool Aid to drink. Even without ice, the drink was refreshing nonetheless. The sugar in the Kool Aid gave such a lift to our tired and thirsty hiker friends. It was so good for Les and me to sit and talk with them about their own language learning experiences. Even though we had lived so diversely, we became a very tight-knit group.

We had rules for the group's first six weeks in the Ifugao province. The first and most difficult rule was that we could not leave our village for any reason (including attending church) other than "life or death". The length of our training time was four months. TAP had made the rules and set goals for us that we were required to meet. The immediate tasks were:

1. Learn the Ayangan (eye YANG un) language.
2. Learn the Ifugao culture.
3. Teach literacy to adults at night (they worked in their rice paddies during the day).
4. Keep a notebook of our daily activities and language learning progress.
5. If time permitted, we could offer any medical help that we felt comfortable in giving. But there was

little time for doing anything other than the four major tasks required by TAP.

Our home was a nipa (NEE pah) hut made of woven bamboo and set on six-foot poles. We had no conveniences such as: running water, furniture, bathrooms, showers, electricity, washers/dryers, or grocery stores. The simplicity of our living conditions proved to be a contradiction in terms. "Simple" usually meant very time consuming. Most of our daily challenges were basic to living:

boiling water for drinking, 2) doing laundry by hand, and 3) learning to cook over an open flame or on the two-burner kerosene stove. With those chores we were kept busily at work especially when factoring in the other requirements and learning tasks. Les and I were determined to work hard and do our very best. Our hearts were in agreement with wanting to please the Lord and not complain about our circumstances or grumble about things we didn't have.

Initially the most difficult thing for us was having no toilet or shower. Our landlord (pah TURN oh) told us that he would be the one to build the outhouse; it took three-weeks before it was built. It had three walls but had no privacy door and no roof. We used our National Airlines umbrella as a "roof." It fit perfectly over the top and was ideal, especially when it rained. Since the umbrella was bright orange and yellow, it was apparent when the facilities were occupied. It faced a deep ravine and was about 100 feet from our hut. Gratefully, no one lived across the ravine from us. The shower was made of woven bamboo walls and within four days was ready for use. Les and our landlord, Paterno, telescoped bamboo poles up at the spring running down to our house. But the shower, like the outhouse, never got a door. It became necessary for Les and me to wait until the village children were in school before taking our showers.

The following stories you are about to read are about our time in Ilap. They are an honest reflection of what God taught us during our unusual and difficult training time. We have marveled at the amazing ways God spoke to us, provided for us and clearly taught us about Himself. We learned that He is absolutely trustworthy, dependable and faithful for every circumstance of life. It is not necessary to become a missionary in order for Him to reveal His character to us. But He does need our attention and our trust in Him. He longs for and desires for us to know Him better. Therefore, we hope the stories and testimonies about our time in Ilap will bless and encourage you. Regardless of where you live or what your circumstances or situations are, God really does want us to see great and mighty things about Himself. Then we can love and trust Him even more.

Psalm 126:3 (NKJV)

*"The Lord has done great things for us,
and we are glad."*

CHAPTER 12
The Borrowed Blanket

Unlike hot and sultry Manila, the area where the FTC course would be taught in the cool and sometimes cold, mountainous, Ifugao province. We had no way of knowing that temperatures dropped considerably after the sun dipped below the mountains in the late afternoon. When I envisioned tropical climates and islands, I never thought in terms of being cold or needing a blanket. A tropical, yet cold, place seemed like another "yo-yo thing" to us.

The two of us landed in Manila in mid-August. Then we caught a bus to Bagabag the next day. The trip was an eight-hour ride to a place near the Ifugao area. We would be joining the other FTC trainees who were awaiting our arrival. There were 12 of us who would spend the next five days together learning valuable information for living in the Ifugao province. We had no idea how to repack our suitcases with all the right things necessary for this FTC. The information we had learned about the Ifugao province helped us decide to take just our jungle camp suitcase; it was already packed and ready to go. We prayed that whatever we were going to need while living in Ifugao would be in that suitcase!

Right before leaving for Ifugao, we decided to add some medicines that we had brought from the States; we put them in Zip-lock bags in our suitcase. And with those things packed to take with us, we felt ready to begin our training in Ifugao.

Ilap, in the Ifugao province, was a beautiful mountain village set in a jungle-like area. It had banana palms and coffee bean trees, as well as other exotic trees unfamiliar to us. It would be our home for the next four months.

Our first two nights in Ilap were cold and miserable. Then I remembered the "sheet blanket." I had packed that blanket before leaving hot Texas. Now I hugged it like a long- lost buddy. And I knew then why God had led me to include that blanket to bring with us! Since it was very thin and light, we thought the blanket would be perfect for Ilap.

Psalm 34:10

"But they that seek the Lord shall not be in want of any good thing."

One day it became necessary for Les and me to make an unscheduled trip to Bagabag to wash and dry our clothes, including the sheet blanket. Although the blanket was thin and light, it also absorbed water and had mildewed. In addition, the blanket, when wet, did not keep us warm.

While in Bagabag, I had mentioned our cold, miserable nights to Margaret Rhoads. She was the very able and competent "Keeper of the Guest House." The Guest House was the place where wayfaring missionaries could stop in, sleep and have a good home-cooked meal.

Margaret was an encouragement to both of us and, at one point, she offered us the use of her "space blanket." Gratefully we accepted her offer. The space blanket, when folded up, reminded me of one of those little plastic rain bonnets for ladies. It fit into a little plastic sleeve about the size of a pack of gum. But when unfolded, the space blanket was the size of a twin-bed sheet. However, the composition of the blanket remained a mystery to us. It had the appearance of ultra-thin foil, except that it was soft and pliable. The blanket had a rich look about it, one side being silver and the other metallic gold.

Finally, after much discussion with Margaret, we left the Guest House. With our backpacks filled with fresh laundry and armed with the space blanket, we made our way back to Ilap. Les and I would now be able to share the space blanket to help keep us warm at night. We were confident that our problem of being cold at night had at last been solved.

On a particularly cold, rainy and windy night, Les and I decided that it was the perfect time to use our borrowed space blanket. We went through our usual routine of setting up the mosquito netting. At last we fell upon our mattress and covered ourselves with the space blanket. Crackle, crunch, crackle! I began to giggle. With every move we made (even breathing), the space blanket made noises. It was as if we were sleeping in a giant bed of Rice Krispies after the milk had been added. We couldn't bat an eyelash without hearing the noisy "snap, crackle and pop" all around us!

We considered our options. We could either be:

1. warm and awake, using the borrowed space blanket;
2. cold and awake, without using the blanket; or
3. warm and asleep, using the blanket but neither of us daring to move a muscle the entire night.

Ultimately, it was clear that the noisy space blanket, while keeping us warm, also would keep us awake all night!

The following day we carefully refolded the space blanket and returned it to its little plastic sleeve for return to Margaret. Her thoughtfulness in lending us her blanket was warming to our hearts at least. However, neither Les nor I will ever forget our dilemma over the use of the borrowed space blanket.

2 Timothy 2:3 (NIV)

"Endure hardship with us like a good soldier of Christ Jesus."

CHAPTER 13
The Butterfly Tree

Some people mistakenly believe that the life of a missionary is one of only hard work and self-sacrifice with very little beauty or fun. You would be only half-right. It is a life of self-sacrifice and hard work. The big surprise for me was to see how God rewarded us with incredible beauty, wonderful new friends and lots of fun while serving Him as missionaries.

We were assigned to serve in administrative jobs with WBT in Manila. We were called support missionaries, not translators. Before Les and I married, I had lived in Africa as a missionary. I was already aware of the cultural, religious, and dietary differences, but that was not the case with Les. It would be his first time to live in a cross-cultural situation.

We were asked to be part of an experiment to train with the national Bible translation group. We arrived in Manila during a typhoon with jet lag and blood-shot eyes. That was due to the nineteen-hour airplane trip and no sleep. We were not the most alert couple for that eight-hour indoctrination by the national translation group, but physically, we were present. Afterwards, we were shuttled onto a big bus for a six-hour ride to the region called Nueva Vizcaya (nu WAVE ah vis KAI ya). Of course, it rained all the way there. Nueva Vizcaya was where the Bagabag Center of WBT was located. But it was still on the large island of Luzon. We arrived late in the night and were met by Winston and Lois Churchill, who are Canadians and also with WBT). We had been assigned to be their prayer partners while we trained in Ilap. It was in their house that we stayed our first night there.

Les and I, along with the other trainees, stayed in Bagabag for about five days. Our purpose during that time was to gather more information, training and instructions. After our time of training there, we were loaded into vans to begin our training in the mountains of the Ifugao area. Ifugao can mean both a mountainous area of Luzon and a particular ethnic or tribal people.

But getting to Ilap was interesting for Les and me. Leaving Bagabag, all of the trainees were loaded into vans. We drove north for about 45 minutes, passing villages and houses made of cinder block. But the farther we traveled, the more jungle we saw and fewer people. Finally, we stopped by the roadside and parked all of the vans. "Honestly," I thought, "Okay, where is Ilap?" Just then, we were told to gather all of our earthly possessions to begin the long hike to Ilap. Ilap, true to its name, sat on top of the mountain. That name began to make more sense as we arduously climbed the mountain with our arms and our backpacks filled with our belongings. With boxes filled with supplies and our overstuffed backpacks, it made the trip exhausting. I'm sure that those two, red-faced Americans were the talk of all the villagers as we passed them, huffing, puffing and plodding on to Ilap. It was not a proper trail, only a carabao (CARE a bough) or water buffalo path. Later, I would be surprised to see just how beautiful the area was when we had passed on our journey there. We were so focused on trying to make it to the top of the mountain that our thoughts were not on our beautiful surroundings; it was on breathing and our screaming muscles.

Ginger and Les' new home

After about an hour's climb, we arrived at our destination—our home for the next four months of training. There it stood on six-foot poles. A ladder was required to get inside that little shanty made of woven bamboo with its thatched roof. There were four doors but no windows in the house. It was just one big (12-foot by 14-foot) room. And it was totally empty except for an open fire pit. The interior was black caused by smoke from cooking in the open fire pit. I knew I would need to learn to cook over the open fire; it was a far cry from my automatic gas range back home in Dallas. I knew my biggest battle facing me would be the fire pit! And of course, the real test was in trying to keep the fire lit. There was a time when I took off my big, straw hat to fan the flames when suddenly I noticed my hat was on fire! Doing "The Mexican Hat Dance" atop my big floppy hat did put out the flames, but it did nothing to enhance its appearance. Afterwards, my hat looked as if a giant had taken a huge bite from the brim. Surely though, with my hat as unexpected kindling, it was the best fire I ever had! But my hat lost its southern charm.

Before leaving for Ilap, Les and I had been warned to take bug spray with us. It turned out to be great advice! Shortly after we arrived in our new home, we closed the place up. Then we set the spray to go off to kill whatever was living inside the hut. Outside our nipa hut, we sat on a log and waited for the spray to work its magic. My prayer was that it would do a very thorough job. Night was coming in just a few hours and we needed to sleep there. I wanted ALL of the varmints dead!

Later, when we opened the doors of our hut, Les and I couldn't believe the collection of insects lying on the floor. I didn't know spiders grew that big; some were as large as my hand. Nor did I know cockroaches could manage to fly while dying! It seemed that every kind of insect in Ilap was supersized! I'm not a soothsayer or a seer, but I could see "the handwriting on those bamboo walls!" It became apparent to me that our lives were going to be VERY interesting in the days and months to come. And I was not wrong!

Eventually, we settled into our nipa hut home, becoming more comfortable living there. It was a simpler life with no running water, no electricity, no furniture (can you believe, nothing to dust?), and no indoor plumbing. It may have been simple by those standards, but maintaining that simple life took a lot of hard work.

Les became my "running" water as he carried our water from the spring to our hut. Then we needed to boil the water before filtering it. Only after that was it fit for drinking.

Doing our laundry by hand (Les was my "wringer-outer") was laborious, exhausting, as well as time-consuming. Adjustment and adaptation were key words for our lives. Also, learning to be grateful for what we DID have, while not thinking about what was missing, became our focus. It took our conscious effort to set our thoughts aside, choosing not to become negative about them. Our nextdoor neighbors were Christians and were wonderful people. They were helpful and gracious but they didn't speak English. Their son Leon, an agricultural student in college, did speak some English. Consequently, Leon was a big help to us as we endeavored to establish ourselves there. Actually, it was Leon's house we occupied. He moved back home with his parents so that we could have a place to live. There were no rent houses in Ilap.

Leon's parents, Colem and Paterno, had a prayer group that met on Wednesday nights. The Paternos invited Les and me to attend. Neither of us knew a single word of the Ayangan language, but still we wanted to attend their prayer meeting. After all, wasn't our God the God of all languages?

About dark, we all met in Paterno's yard where a big fire had been built to TRY to keep the mosquitoes away.

We sat around the fire on stumps and logs while the Paternos served coffee to their guests. There we were—two Americans sitting in the dark with only the fire to give us light. There may have been six or seven others present besides the Paternos, Les and me.

I want to stress this was not the instant variety of coffee that the Paternos served. That coffee grew in our yard just outside our hut and all along the mountain trails near us. The coffee was freshly ground, mountain-grown and STRONG. I declined the coffee because I was not supposed to have caffeine, but Les drank some. Afterwards, for three long nights Les didn't sleep at all. His heart raced and pounded from drinking just one cup of the 100% pure, mountain-grown coffee. Obviously, his American body was not used to the REAL deal!

I watched the sparks from the fire flying up into the inky blackness of the sky as zillions of stars showed huge and bright. And since we were on the other side of the world, we were seeing different constellations. It confirmed to us that even the heavens seemed foreign to us. I sat there and thought to myself, "God, what in the world am I doing here in this tiny remote village? I feel so alienated from anything familiar to me. The people, their language and culture are so different from my own friends and family. Show me YOURSELF in the midst of all this foreignness which I'm experiencing now." Those were some of my thoughts as I whispered my prayer to Him while sitting by the fire that night. Les and I listened while our brothers and sisters in Christ verbalized their needs to our God in their own Ayangan language. It was a moment in time that we will never forget.

Then I looked up and I saw it! Behind the fire stood a magnificent, flowering tree. I had not noticed the tree before that moment. It was totally alight with fireflies, shining and blinking in the night. Later, I asked our host friends, "What is the name of that tree?" Leon told us, "It is called a butterfly orchid tree." Can you imagine sitting there in complete awe of God who had just allowed me to view such a lovely sight? It reminded me in some small way of the "fairy lights" at Disneyland. I was mesmerized watching the lighted tree as its "lights" blinked on and off. How absolutely perfect and what a faithful God to bring such beauty to us as we watched the tree lighting up the entire area of our neighbor's yard.

Later that night while lying upon our mattress on the floor, these were some of my thoughts and impressions because of God's firefly show that night:

1. God knew exactly where we were.
2. He knew why we were in Ilap.
3. He reminded me of His great love for us via the beautiful show of lights.
4. Also, He wanted us to see just how big He is. And how big is that?
5. Big enough to handle any situation which might present itself to us.
6. Lastly, if He could control the fireflies in a tree, He could control anything!

I felt His peace flood my soul as I reflected on His awareness of us. One thing was certain. If I had not opened my heart and eyes, I would have missed seeing His blessings, His faithfulness and His provisions for us.

That night was the beginning of many lessons God would teach us as we learned to trust Him in obscure and remote Ilap.

Psalm 32:8

"I will instruct you and teach you in the way that you should go; I will counsel you with My eye upon you."

CHAPTER 14
Searching for a Quiet Place

It was a fine day in Ilap in the Ifugao mountain province. The sun shone brightly, the air was clean, except for the pungent smells of the flowering trees next to our hut. We were new to that area of the Philippines and I was trying to re-establish a pattern that would help me keep my daily appointment with the Lord. And so I began my search for a similar quiet place in Ilap.

Psalm 145:18

"The Lord is near to all who call upon Him, to all who call upon Him in truth."

It had been my daily habit for the past 10 to 12 years to have "quiet time" with the Lord. It had always been the first thing I would do in the morning. I would take my Bible, devotional book and spiral notebook to record my prayers, praises and requests and find a place to meet with God. However, since arriving in Ilap, there were just too many demands on my time early in the morning. Thus, I opted to change the order of my morning routine. I did not want to feel rushed in my meeting with the Lord.

Flexibility is not the only key to living the life of a missionary, but it is an important one. I felt good about the change I had made and my resolve to do it; my heart was glad.

While looking for the perfect place to meet with the Lord, I spotted a small hill in the back of our nipa hut. I thought to myself, "Now that is the perfect place!" It had a grand view of the deep ravine and mountains surrounding us. I found a place to sit and brushed away the loose rocks and small gravel. But I had made sure that I was not about to sit on an anthill or some type of varmint. I sat down and got comfortable to begin my time with the Lord. Now I finally had a workable and livable solution to the problem of finding a quiet place—or so I thought.

I had sat there only for a few minutes when Leon, our 18-year old neighbor, came over to where I was sitting. I thought to myself, "No Lord, I want to be ALONE with You!"

Leon said to me, "Ma'am, you're sitting on my uncle." "Excuse me? I'm sorry, Leon," I said, "I think I misunderstood what you just said to me; please repeat it for me."

Once again he said to me, "Where you are now sitting is the place where we buried my uncle."

Why is it that graves have such ghoulish effects upon us poor mortals? The truth was that this mortal moved much faster than ever before! I was off that grave in a flash. Not one time afterwards did I ever have any desire to go sit on that little hill again. It was much too quiet there, anyway. And so my search for a quiet place continued.

James 4:8

"Draw near to God and He will draw near to you..."

CHAPTER 15
Green Beans and Other Miracles

When Les and I volunteered to go to Ilap, we were unaware of all the history surrounding us. The Ifugao people had at one time been known as headhunters.

During WWII while the Japanese occupied the Philippine Islands, they were very much afraid of the fierce Ifugao people. Les and I were shown caves and hiding places used by the Japanese. In fact, the area was still saturated with war memorabilia left behind by the Japanese. Our focus at that time was struggling to get belongings, our supplies and ourselves to Ilap. After a lot of sweating, hard work and several rest stops, we made it to our new home, a nipa hut with a ladder to get inside it.

The trainee group was divided into groups of two. Each group was given a whole sack of rice since Filipinos ate more rice than Americans. Consequently, Les and I were given a half sack of rice (about 25 pounds). That was supposed to last us six weeks or through the end of our testing time. Then we would be free to leave our area to replenish our supplies. The training time was to simulate what Bible translators experience when they go into a new area to translate God's Word. In the meantime, the group would meet at designated times and places for our outdoor training experiences. We would all be notified of any such meeting. During the outdoor training times, the group learned about the vegetation/foods of our area. The purpose was to teach us how to supplement our mainly rice diets with available foods growing around us.

Les and I did okay with our rice and the few rations we had brought in our backpacks. We had cans of tuna, Spam, peanut butter and Cheese Whiz. Also, we had brought along a tin of crackers, some oatmeal, tea, coffee, sugar, flour, oil, baking powder, and soap to launder our clothes.

As you know, the best-laid plans don't always go as planned. I had never before shopped for a six-weeks' supply of food. How could I know that we didn't have enough?

Somewhere around week four and a half I knew that we wouldn't make our six-week target date with the food allowances. I went to Les and explained our problem. After a lengthy discussion, we both agreed we could NOT leave our assigned area. As the oldest members in the group, the younger team members looked to us as their example; we could not let them down.

Les and I decided to pray about our foodless situation. We began to do that at dinner. Our evening meal was this: Les would eat four crackers with peanut butter and I would eat my two with Cheese Whiz on them. He had coffee and I had hot tea. It was cold at night up in Ilap and it was a nice ending to our day to have hot drinks with our dinner meal. As we prayed that evening, we asked God to help us be the people He wanted us to be. Meanwhile, we admitted to Him that we had a problem—we were almost foodless.

We did have a little flour and a bit of oil and rice. After we had prayed together and just before closing up our doors for the night, I noticed a small bundle of green beans neatly tied together with a piece of grass lying in our doorway. Where in the world did they come from and who put the beans there? We were never sure how the green beans arrived in our doorway, but that was not the point. The point was that now we had rice AND green beans. We rejoiced and praised God for His faithfulness.

Bedtime was a frustrating, time-consuming ordeal all its own and it all had to do with the mosquito netting. That was necessary because malaria, the type that caused the brain to swell, was prevalent in our area. Les hung the netting by ropes over one of the beams overhead and balanced it using bamboo poles. The poles went through loops on the four corners of the netting.

THEN the netting must be tucked in around our mattress on the floor to keep the mosquitoes and a host of other creepy, crawly things from getting inside. Every night we struggled with all the obstacles that needed to be overcome in setting up the netting. Then, exhausted, we would finally fall upon our bed on the floor. It was our usual habit after retiring to our mattress on the floor that we prayed together. That night we focused on our need for food. Neither of us had been in a situation where we had no food. And fresh on our hearts was our praise to God for how He had brought us the green beans to go with our rice. Just as we had uttered those words of praise to God, we heard someone call my name. "Ginger, it's me.

Open the door." I got out of bed, found my flashlight and opened the door. There stood Marie, my language helper. "I killed a chicken and I wanted to share it with you," Marie explained. I thanked her profusely for the chicken. Then Marie and I said our good nights and she returned to her home.

Because we had no refrigeration, I took a bit of flour and oil and cooked the two chicken legs and thighs Marie had brought us. I assessed our situation and realized that we now had rice, fried chicken and green beans. It was a virtual feast for us. I returned to bed and again we praised God for His mercies and for His provisions. A wonderful meal was awaiting us the next day.

Early the next morning, I noticed that the papaya given to us more than a week before had ripened overnight. The papaya would be added to our meal, making it well-balanced by our western standards.

I began snapping the green beans when I heard a booming American voice and I knew it was not Les who was speaking! Les had gone to the spring to get our water in a bamboo tube. I wondered, "Who in the world could be talking with Les and in English, too?" I leaned out the door and saw Don Leonard, a Lutheran pastor we had met the year before. He was also with WBT. We had met Don and his wife Pam when we trained together at the University of Oklahoma. We had not seen them since that time.

Don was about 6'5" tall, a giant of a man (not just in stature but spiritually, too). It was just too wonderful to see him. We asked him to sit with us on one of the logs outside our house to catch up on all the news. Having

Don hike up to see us was like a breath of fresh air for Les and me. We were hungry to see a friend and one who spoke our language as well. Les and I invited Don to stay and share our meal with us. After all, we had four pieces of fried chicken, rice, papaya and green beans.

I left Les to talk with Don while I went to put the finishing touches on our meal. There was just enough flour to make gravy to go with the rice and chicken. Surveying the chicken and gravy, plus the green beans and papaya, it was apparent to me that the Lord had prepared a feast for us. And God had brought Don Leonard to share it with us.

Shortly after our arrival in Ilap, Les had made us a rectangular table that was the height of a coffee table. It was there that the three of us sat cross-legged on the floor to eat our meal. When it came time to bless the food, Les began to praise God for our food. But he became too emotional to finish. Then I tried to finish what Les had begun, but I too began to weep. Don finished thanking God for our food. Then he said to us, "Okay, tell me what has happened." We began to share our food situation and to recount the ways that God had answered our prayers. It was an emotional time for the three of us to "see" and "taste" that holy meal which God had prepared for us.

When Don was ready to leave, he reached into his Ifugao backpack and said, "Ginger, Pam sent this to you." There Don stood with a box similar to a large shoebox and beautifully gift wrapped. But as Don was leaving, he asked us to wait until he was gone before we opened it. Les walked with Don all the way down the mountain to the place Don had parked his car. Then Les hiked about another hour back to our house.

I could hardly wait for Les' return so we could open the box. After he arrived, we sat on the floor and opened the gift. We were stunned by the contents of the box! It was as if Pam had known everything about our situation. The box was filled with food! Pam had packed the box with Pringles potato chips, a box of Kraft macaroni and cheese, a can of tuna fish, a can of Spam, and a block of Kraft cheese that needed no refrigeration. There were crackers, a jar of stuffed olives and a package of Hershey miniature candies. NO one knew that Les' favorite candy was semi-sweet chocolate or that mine was "Mr.

Goodbar;" that is, no one but GOD! Les and I both wept together at the incredible way God had answered our prayers. God had provided more than enough food to last until the six week testing time was over. And He sent one of His own precious children, Don, to deliver it and to speak encouraging words to us. What an awesome, dependable, giving, and loving God we serve!

Neither Les nor I will ever forget that time when God's provisions for us were wrapped in love and hand-delivered in a shoebox by Don, one of His choice representatives. "To God goes all the glory, great things He has done!"

Matthew 6:25-26 (NIV)

"Therefore I tell you, do not worry about your life, what you will eat or drink; or about your body, what you will wear. Is not your life more important than food, and the body more important than clothes? Look at the birds of the

air; they do not sow or reap or store away in barns, and yet your heavenly Father feeds them. Are you not much more valuable than they?"

CHAPTER 16
More Than Rice

There was only one way to arrive in Ilap and that was to hike up the mountain by a carabao trail. Most of the trail was only five or six feet wide. But there were places where it narrowed even more, making our journey more difficult, especially when we carried our supplies.

Ginger and Les; in back are the Banaue Rice Terraces

Often I wished that I could fully enjoy the trek to Ilap because the area was truly beautiful with dark green vegetation. Tall, Ipil Ipil (EE pil EE pil) trees native to the Philippines surrounded us.

There was a host of familiar-looking plants growing along the sides of the trails, plants we had only seen in floral shops.

Mother-in-law tongues grew wild there. Back in the States, I had admired those for years and the Ifugao mountain sides were alive with their beauty.

Climbing the trail to Ilap for Les and me was exhausting. We rarely talked to each other during our hike; talking took too much energy. We tried to carry little with us to Ilap. But in doing so we got ourselves into a bind. I had never had to purchase enough food to last us six weeks. That period of time was the first stage of our training. Part of our training was learning to stay put in Ilap. I thought the twenty-five pounds of rice we had left would be enough. It seemed like a lot of rice to us. We had hoped it would carry us through the testing time. However, five weeks into our training, we began to run out of food, except for a little rice! Even though the rice had bugs in it, I knew I could get rid of them by washing the rice before cooking it. After all, I reasoned, rice might get boring, but it would be enough.

In the evenings by lantern light, it became my habit to write thank-you letters to our family, financial partners and our prayer supporters. Raymond and Barbara McKee received a letter from us during the time of the "green bean miracle." Late in October, we received a package from them. After Raymond received our letter, he became very burdened about our food situation. Back when Les and I lived in Conroe, Texas, Raymond and Barbara lived in an adjoining neighborhood. Also, for several years we attended the same church. Our children were the same ages and they attended church camp together. Barbara and Raymond were friends who knew our lifestyle and us. Our lives in Ilap bore no similarities to what Barbara and Raymond had observed previously. I think they were concerned for us. Raymond was moved in his heart to do something to help us.

It was a dark and stormy night (I've always wanted to write those words)! Regardless of what else Raymond wanted to do that night in Conroe, he could not get us off his mind. He tried to sleep, but that didn't work! He had managed to delay what he felt that he should do until three o'clock in the morning. By that time the storm was intense with lightning, thunder and rain coming down in torrents. Even that did not deter Raymond from getting out of bed, dressing and driving to the only grocery store open in the city at that hour. Aisle by aisle Raymond maneuvered his cart through the store. He chose items that required no refrigeration, but would still be nourishing. After making all of his purchases, he drove home, boxed up everything and mailed the package that day via AIRMAIL!

On the other side of the world, it was dark when our FTC leader Nel Binayao (be NIGH yo) arrived at our nipa hut. On his shoulder Nel had carried a very large box up the mountain to us. We could barely contain our excitement when we saw the box. Though it was only October, it was like Christmas for the two of us. We thanked Nel for delivering the box to us and then Nel left to return to his own home.

We were well aware of God's faithfulness to us in caring for our needs; we had experienced it before with the green bean miracle. So it was a tearful and emotional experience for us as we carefully unwrapped the box. We understood that when God sends you a package, it becomes a holy moment.

The array of edibles in the box was staggering to us. It was apparent to Les and me that Raymond's selections had been carefully made. As we removed each item from the box, we wept. Raymond remembered that we had no electricity and he had chosen food items that needed no refrigeration. The "Butter Buds," included were the PERFECT solution for our living situation. That choice gave us something that tastes like butter, yet, didn't need refrigeration. I could mix the exact amount needed without wasting any of it.

Neither Les nor I had EVER heard of "Butter Buds," but Raymond knew and he had included that particular treasure in our box. Other selections made by Raymond delighted us and gave us a variety of ways to change our monotonous diet. The instant mashed potatoes were a pleasant change from our strictly rice diet. But the cans of chili (Texas food), gravy mixes, cans of chicken and beef put smiles on both of our faces. Other things Raymond and Barbara included blessed us then and in the days to come. Every time we chose something to eat that they had sent us, it reminded us once more of God's faithful provisions for ALL of our needs.

Lamentations 3:22-23

"...For His compassions never fail. They are new every morning; Great is Thy faithfulness."

The beautiful example demonstrated by Raymond and Barbara shows us how the body of Christ functions; it was monumental to Les and me. It all began when Raymond listened to God speaking to him. But obedience was the key to what God had laid on their hearts. Les and I were able to see, taste and experience God's faithful provisions for us by giving us more than rice through our brother and sister in Christ.

1 Corinthians 12:12-13, 26

"For even as the body is one and yet has many members, and all the members of the body, though they are many, are one body, so also is Christ. And if one member suffers, all the members suffer with it; if one member is honored, all the members rejoice with it."

CHAPTER 17
Never Trust a Rock in the River

Because our training group had been told by our leader Nel Binayao, not to leave our places for six weeks, which proved to be a difficult and stretching time for us. Therefore, since we were not even allowed to attend church, Les and I had church in our own little nipa hut. Worshiping God does not require buildings, stained glass windows, pipe organs, pianos, choirs, or graduate seminary pastors. It was Les and me alone with GOD! It was a new experience for us. We began our worship time by reading some of the Psalms. Then we sang, praised the Lord and prayed together. Each of our worship services was different, but each one was a sweet time worshiping the Lord, those first six weeks living in Ilap. We could sense God moving us into a closer relationship with Himself.

When that first part of our restricted training ended, the two of us decided to attend a tiny church down the mountain from us. The church was very close to the main road and the place to which we were brought on that first day. It seemed strange to be going somewhere where there were people, especially other Christians. We prepared to make our trek down the mountain carrying our Ifugao backpack, our Bibles and water to drink. It had rained the night before, which complicated our walk down the mountain. As we left our village, the small groups of people became a virtual stream of "people traffic." They joined us on our walk to church. That "companion society" for which the Filipinos were well known was living up to its name. We all looked like ducks as we walked in a row, delicately making our way down the muddy mountain trail.

A really cute little gal walked ahead of me and I began to follow in her footsteps. She was dressed very fashionably and had on pretty white shoes. I thought to myself, "Good luck with the white shoes, girl!" She was very petite. Carefully she placed her dainty little feet as she walked down the slippery mountain trail. I followed her every step as I put my feet into her footprints. My own sneakers were a muddy mess and we hadn't been walking 10 minutes. But her shoes were still WHITE; I wondered how she could have managed that.

After a time, we came to a small stream. It was not deep, but still it must be crossed. It was about a 75-foot span across the stream to the other side. I thought to myself, "How are we going to traverse that?" But the "white-shoed" girl began to place her feet on the rocks that were scattered across the stream. I followed her step for step. Les followed me along in my steps, choosing those same rocks. I was about to sigh a big sigh of relief in reaching the other side of the stream unscathed. Then I stepped on the big, flat rock that the white-shoed girl had just walked on. But when my American-sized body landed on the rock, it flipped up and over. I did remember seeing a huge rock coming toward my face and I instinctively turned my head! And I fell headlong into the icy mountain stream, hitting my thigh on the rock.

I felt as though I'd lost a bout with Mohammed Ali! The icy cold water was a jolt to my entire body. Since I had seen the rock coming toward me, I had managed to twist my body enough to keep my face and head out of harm's way. But that was not true of my left side. My left leg and thigh hurt so badly that I cried. Les was standing knee- deep in the stream trying to help me stand up. I was embarrassed because I had fallen and I was sopping wet. Now I would have to sit through church in my disheveled, muddied and painful condition. Already I was one cold, hurting hunk of humiliated humanity.

We could see the church from where we stood in the water. Les helped me as I hobbled toward the church; I was in great pain. I had worn slacks and there was no place to go to assess the damage done to my leg. We walked into the church and sat down. People stared at me as I sat dripping water onto the floor. The pews were only boards placed on upended logs. Since the church service was all in Ayangan, Les and I only understood the word "Jesus" (hay SOOS). I sat in pain, but praised the Lord that I was not hurt as badly as I could have been. A serious head injury or a broken bone could have resulted in our being forced to leave our training group. I DID NOT WANT THAT TO HAPPEN! So I praised God for His protection from a worse situation.

After the church service ended, Les and I began the long, slow and painful walk back to our nipa hut. Normally, it was an hour's walk, but on that Sunday it took us much longer. At last we arrived back at our hut. There I was able to assess the damage done by that rock in the river.

I LOVE the color purple! Actually, purple and green were two of my favorite colors. But those two colors were not necessarily good colors for skin tones. Maybe it was good that I liked those colors since I'd be wearing them for quite some time. I had a huge angry hematoma on my thigh; it was about the size of a large grapefruit or pomelo. Les thought I needed to seek medical help. But after discussing it, we thought we should wait a day or so before we made that decision. The next morning my swollen and bruised thigh felt hot. I took some aspirin and rested all day. After three days, I was able to maneuver up and down the ladder and I was able to carry on most of my daily routine. We had NOT had to leave and seek medical help. I felt blessed by the Lord in my improvement. I never saw the white-shoed girl again. Quite honestly, I don't blame her for staying away from me. Had I been in her shoes, I would have stayed as far away from me as possible. But it was unfortunate that I didn't see her again; I had a question that I really wanted to ask her. Did she have some Ifugao secret for keeping her white shoes clean on a muddy trail? Now, I would never know!

Thessalonians 5:16-18 (NIV)

"Be joyful always; pray continually, give thanks in all circumstances, for this is God's will for you in Christ Jesus."

CHAPTER 18
What Fellowship Has Light With Darkness?

With our conservative church backgrounds, Les and I had read about spiritual warfare in the Bible and only experienced a little of it while on our trip to Ethiopia.

But we had never come so blatantly face to face with it before our Ilap adventure.

Our TAP group consisted of men and women who had felt God's call to be personally involved in Bible translation work. Their heart's desire was to see God's Word made available to all the indigenous people in their own language within their own country. Les and I felt it an honor to be a part of that new venture with them.

Part of the program for us was to teach literacy classes. It was one of the requirements that became our focus. In addition, we had many other daily duties and responsibilities. All of our laundry had to be done by hand. Much of our time was consumed with just trying to keep water boiled for drinking. But being thirsty and waiting for hot water to cool were not always compatible. Then there was the need to "hold" clinic every day (sometimes two or three times a day) and that took up much of our time also. The needs of the people who came for help were staggering. At other times while I'd be "doctoring" someone's wound, I'd be praying silently, "Lord, please let me do this patient no harm." Then there were other occasions, as I treated a person, I would be weeping over their pain and suffering. I could NEVER be a doctor, but I did have a lot of sympathy and compassion—maybe more than I needed!

Literacy classes, primarily for older adults, were taught in the one-room schoolhouse. It was very basic with tables, benches and a blackboard. The only fly in the ointment was that it was necessary to wait until night to teach the classes. This was because both men and women needed to work all day in the rice fields.

The purpose for teaching a literacy class was really two-fold:

1) to learn to read God's Word in their own language, and
2) to sign their names in cursive writing for legal documents, voting and correspondence.

In Ilap there was no electricity anywhere, including the school. Consequently, we took our borrowed Coleman lantern with us to use for light. Coleman lanterns, which require wicks called "mantles," must also be pumped full of air to burn brightly. For the older folk who had visual problems, it was especially important to have good lighting. And our Coleman lantern provided that.

Before leaving our nipa hut, Les tested our lantern to be sure that it was in good working order. Then we began our walk further up the mountain to the schoolhouse.

With no source of light except our flashlight, our walk up the narrow trail to the school was a dark one. Few houses we passed showed any light burning inside them. At times when we turned to look back across the dark mountains, we could see the bobbing of lights along the mountain trail. More than likely, they were members of our class hurrying to our literacy lessons.

I never dreamed that teaching literacy to adults would cause the spirit world to become actively involved in our efforts. But that is apparently what happened. Initially our classes went really well. The first class seemed easy for us and the students were enthusiastic about learning to read and write. The lantern burned beautifully. Going home that first night, Les and I felt moderately successful. The next week we again tested the lantern before we left home. It was okay—until we got to the school. Then despite all our efforts, we could not get the lantern to work. Some of the men probably thought it was because the two Americans were unfamiliar with operating the lantern. But when they tried to make the lantern work, it refused to burn for them as well. The local "chief" sent a young boy back to his own home in the village to get his Coleman lantern. A few minutes later, the boy returned to the school with the chief's lantern. But just like our lantern, his refused to burn as well. That night there was a lot of chatter among the students about the lantern dilemma!

It was disheartening for Les and me to have our class sitting in the dark waiting patiently for us to get our act together. The people had worked hard all day in the rice paddies. But despite all our efforts, the lantern refused to burn. Les worked tirelessly on the lantern. I was "sweating bullets" as I watched him trying to figure out why the lantern had refused to burn. Even though several of us had brought flashlights, there was just not enough light to teach reading and writing. Some of our adult students were so poor that they had brought their homemade lamps. Those lamps were made from Coke bottles filled with kerosene with wicks stuck down inside them. That night we taught our classes by those ineffective lamps; that was how we ended week two.

The third week we changed the mantle in the lantern. We also made sure it had plenty of fuel before we left to teach our class. Along the trail we met the village chief; he too had brought his own Coleman lantern to our literacy class. Now that we had two lanterns, we felt we were "well-covered." Together we made the 10-minute walk to the school. Les was the first to light our lantern. When it lit up, I thought to myself, "Praise God. We will have light to teach our class tonight!" But that was a little premature. Suddenly, our lantern caught fire! Flames shot up to the thatched ceiling and roof. I thought to myself, "We're going to burn down this schoolhouse and everyone will hate us FOREVER!" Les wrapped a jacket around his arm to protect it from the flames and ran outside carrying the flaming lantern with him. There he was able to extinguish the flaming lantern using some sand.

Next, the village chief brought over his lantern and began to do all the necessary things to light it. When it was lit, all of us sighed a huge sigh of relief. But then the chief's lantern caught fire also. Once again Les came to the rescue by carrying the flaming lantern outside to extinguish it.

Dumbfounded by what had just taken place, we stared at each other. Not having adequate light to teach the tired, but faithful, adults frustrated us. That night Les and I returned home, dejected by the night's events. We decided to pray again about the lanterns! But this time we addressed the demonic problem before God. We asked God to fix it. We reminded Him that these were His children who wanted to learn to read His Word. And we needed His supernatural power to accomplish that. Les and I were at WAR—and it was a spiritual battle that we were fighting!

When week four came, we trudged back up the mountain. We had prayed all week that God would be our Victor in our spiritual battle. We wanted to teach those adults who were hungry to read His Word. With our lantern again in hand, we walked to the schoolhouse praying that those adults would not give up in despair and forsake our class. When we arrived, there sat our class with expectant looks on their faces. Those grown men and women were precious people who loved God and belonged to Him. For the most part, the class was composed of Christians. However, the chief and his wife were heavily involved in the animistic world. Calmly, we went through the same procedures required to light the lantern. Our lantern burned brightly and without further incident. We praised God! I was reminded of the verse that says:

John 4:4b

"…Greater is He who is in you than he who is in the world."

We finished our literacy course in Ilap knowing that, had it not been for God's intervention and victory, we could never have done it. Our class members would have remained unlearned, just as Satan wanted them. They would have remained without the skills to read or write. Satan did not want God's children to be able to read His Word! He did not want them to be literate! He wanted them to feel worthless, useless and unable to accomplish God's broader purposes for their lives. But our God is the STRONG ONE. He won the victory in Ilap! Les and I, as well as all the other Christians there who had witnessed those events, knew that to be true.

CHAPTER 19
Dinner With Donny and Marie

We had not been living long in Ilap when our language helper Marie invited us to her home for dinner. She was a schoolteacher and lived not far from the one-room schoolhouse with her husband Donny. Often Les and I laughed about being invited to dinner with Donny and Marie, but the joke remained between us; they had never heard of the Osmonds.

Donny and Marie

The home of Donny and Marie was clean but humble; it had a dirt floor. Donny worked in the post office of Lagawe (la GOW we), the provincial capital. He rode a motorcycle to and from his work; it was the only usable mode of transportation up the mountain to their place. After all, the trail to Ilap was only a carabao trail; it was never meant for vehicular traffic.

Marie and I were standing outside their little house when I saw her chickens. They raised chickens to supplement their diet with the eggs and meat. Schoolteachers in the Philippines, as in the States, do not get much pay. And, at times in the Philippines, some teachers were not paid for months. This was the situation concerning Marie. It was for that reason that Marie and Donny really struggled financially. As we stood there talking, I asked Marie, "What do you feed your chickens?" She smiled and replied, "Oh, they are self-supporting." I think that here in America we would call them "free-range" chickens. I loved her answer and both of us laughed.

We walked back inside the house and sat down in crude wooden chairs. We were waiting for Donny to arrive home from work. It was just before dark when he finally arrived.

About 8:00 in the evening the four of us sat down at their little table. She had used an oilcloth to cover their table and everything was spotlessly clean. Marie started the meal with the one thing that Filipinos always have with their meals—soup. No matter how poor they were, they always began their dinner meal with soup.

That night she served chicken broth in clear glass mugs and in each mug was a chicken foot. It was dark in their home with only a kerosene lamp burning and I prayed my reaction was not noticeable. I just prayed, "Dear God, I just can't eat a chicken foot." I looked at that foot and my mind was in turmoil. My quandary was how not to offend our precious new friends. What was I to do about that chicken foot? I knew better than to offer it to Les; I dared not ask him to eat it. I could see that chicken foot with its toenails still attached, standing in my clear glass mug. There was no telling WHERE that foot had been or what that chicken had walked through! I said to Donny, "I'm not REALLY very hungry tonight, Donny. Would you like to have my chicken foot?" He took it and smiled happily and I knew then he was so glad that I was not really that hungry. Silently I said, "Thank YOU, Jesus, for a very hungry man!"

The remainder of the meal went well and we enjoyed the rest of the chicken, along with rice, of course. We had a good time with Marie and Donny that evening. Les and I wondered, as we walked home that night in the dark, what else did God have in store for us to experience? We were grateful that Donny and Marie were willing to share their very best with us; we praised God for them. Sometimes though, the very best a person has to offer is a chicken foot.

2 Corinthians 12:9 (NKJV)

"My grace is sufficient for you, for my strength is made perfect in weakness."

CHAPTER 20
Helping the Blind to See

In 1982, before Les and I left our home in Conroe, Texas to serve as missionaries in the Philippine Islands, I had begun to have serious problems with my eyes. I was startled to learn that I had corneal ulcers that could endanger my 20/20 vision. If they erupted and were not attended to immediately, I could become blind. Before leaving for the Philippines, I asked my ophthalmologist for all the eye medicine samples he had to take with me; he eagerly complied.

Les and I had been assigned to train in Ilap. It was beautiful area with lush, green, tropical vegetation. It was jungle-like in appearance with the exception of two rolling mountainsides. Those two mountains were completely covered with plants called "mother-in-law tongues" and multi-colored crotons. I'd only seen those in floral shops back in the States. Down the mountainside toward the valley were some of the rice farms. But other rice farms had been carved out of the mountainside and were terraced. Those were similar to the famous Banaue (bah NOW ee) Rice Terraces that had been built by their Ifugao ancestors over a thousand years before. I had "oohed" and "aahed" over such breathtaking views from the top of our mountain until I almost hyperventilated. What an awesome sight to see, literally in my own back yard!

It was surprising to us to learn that most Ifugao people assumed we had formal medical training, but we had none. Les' job was to hand me the correct Zip-lock bag with the appropriate medications inside it as I tried to "doctor" them. Thinking back on the whole medical situation, I had to laugh because we kept all of the medical supplies in three Zip-lock bags. One bag had things needed for bandaging wounds (including gauze, bandages, and cotton swabs). The second bag held gentian violet, sulfa powder, Mercurochrome, Vaseline, and hydrogen peroxide. Those medicines were used to treat scabies, machete cuts, scrapes and burns. All those were very common problems in Ilap. With people cooking over open fires, there were always burns to contend with! The last Zip-lock bag contained aspirin, Lomotil, and some antimalarial medication. Les had purchased a few other medications hoping they would be useful in our village; he was right on target! Because most Ifugao people had taken very little medication during their lifetime, a simple aspirin would cure many of their maladies. Truly, it worked like a wonder drug.

But my "medical" background was nothing more than my life experiences as a mom with tons of BAND-AIDS and Mercurochrome. Raising two children had helped me garner some practical knowledge that proved to be very helpful in Ilap. Perhaps my interest in medicine came from my grandfather who was a doctor. But there was such a need for a person having even the simplest knowledge of medicine. With my practical knowledge using BAND-AIDS, I was the only person in the village who could help them. I was put to the test many times as my day began with a line of people queuing up outside our nipa hut. Holding clinic became part of our normal routine. The difficulty for us was when a person's need went far beyond mere BAND-AIDS! During those times, we felt totally inadequate!

One evening, just as it was getting dark, our 18-year-old neighbor Leon brought a young woman named Carmen to me. Her head and eyes were covered with a dirty rag. I felt terrified by what I might see when I uncovered her head. The only light I had was an impotent flashlight. Since it was impossible for me to try to determine her problem without adequate lighting, I asked him to have her return early the following morning when the sun was shining brightly. Because Carmen spoke no English, Leon was my translator.

As I opened our bamboo door early the next morning, there stood Leon and Carmen waiting for me. When I uncovered Carmen's head, I was shocked to see clusters or a ring of ulcers around BOTH corneas; they were VISIBLE to the naked eye. Normally, a person could not see them without special equipment. I knew the amount of pain she was experiencing! Tears of sympathy and compassion rolled down my face as I stared at the ulcers. Having ulcers on a cornea would be similar to having a crack in a camera lens. It would allow too much light into the eye. The result would be blinding headaches and sunlight would be almost unbearable for one with corneal ulcers. I had wondered how Carmen could bear working in her fields under the bright noonday sun.

I asked Les for my personal medications (in yet another Zip-lock bag). I removed the medication my doctor in Conroe had given to me. It was the newest medicine for her (our) condition. I had Leon explain to Carmen how imperative it was for her to come to me three times each day for treatment. If she did not have the medicine in her eyes regularly, she could go blind. She said she understood and we agreed on the plan of treatment. After applying the medicine, I covered one of her eyes but did not cover the other. She needed to be able to see to get home. She must return in 24 hours so that I could remove that patch and put a clean one on the other affected eye.

When Carmen left, Leon said, "Ma'am, Carmen is the only Christian living in the village. She has been persecuted for her faith. She has two very small children, one an infant. Her husband is not a believer in Christ. She works long, hard hours in her fields and in her rice paddies. Ma'am, she is only 20 years old."

I returned to our little nipa hut after Leon left and prayed. I asked God for a miracle for that young Christian mother and wife, that precious child of His. I asked God to make Carmen a visible example of His mighty, healing power. I prayed that her faith would be made stronger. Then I prayed that her unbelieving husband would have his own spiritual eyes opened. What a testimony Carmen could be for the entire animistic (spirit-worshipping) village!

Carmen came for treatment the first two days and she came three times each day, just as we had agreed. I was feeling confident that she understood the gravity of her situation. On morning three, I waited for her to come for her treatment, but she didn't come. Another hour passed but still no Carmen. I grabbed my medication bag and started off to the village; I had to find her! Up the mountain and through the brushy jungle I hurried. The village was not that far away, maybe 10 to 15 minutes from where we lived.

There was nothing really defining about the village of Ilap. The houses were typical of most Ifugao villages and were built very close together. The nipa huts were made of strips of woven bamboo and all had thatched roofs. But their huts were much smaller than the nipa hut Les and I shared. And while ours was five to six feet off the ground on poles, theirs were only three feet off the ground. That discovery surprised me. I had thought all the nipa huts were built high off the ground like ours.

Walking to the village, I had to wind my way through the pigs, chickens and dogs. I'm not usually afraid of animals, but my hope was that none of the dogs would bite me. After all, I did look different from the people they normally saw. And I was fairly certain that none of those dogs had been vaccinated against rabies! Still, as I walked through the village I was impressed by its cleanliness. The entire area was well swept until the ground was as hard as concrete. Everything in the village appeared neat and orderly.

I had no idea where Carmen lived but as I walked through the village, I called her name. At last, someone led me to her house. Carmen was very embarrassed to learn I had walked to the village on her account. After doctoring her eyes, we chatted for a moment. After having exhausted my entire Ayangan vocabulary of eight or 10 words, I returned home. But from that day forward, Carmen always came to our house at the agreed time.

Six days into her eye treatment, Carmen came to me again. I had asked Leon to ask her how she was doing. Carmen told Leon she couldn't see out of one of her eyes. My heart sank as I asked her, "Not at all?" Leon asked Carmen again but she replied, "Only very little." Once again I doctored her eyes and she left to return to work in her rice paddy.

Back in our nipa hut I cried out to the Lord, "Oh, Father," I begged Him, "You can't let Carmen become blind! Your testimony to her husband and all those animistic villagers is at stake. She needs to be your walking, talking, seeing testimony! The villagers need to see your great power and authority, even over blindness." I praised Him then for His answer to my prayer. The decision for Carmen's vision lay in the hands of the Great Physician. I trusted Him to do what was best for her. I was reminded of this verse:

Genesis 18:14

"Is anything too difficult for the Lord?"

Here's the rest of Carmen's story: Carmen was healed! Her sight was returned and she was able to testify to the village of God's healing powers. What an awesome answer to our prayers for Carmen!

But there was another blessing in my experience with Carmen's eye problems. It was separate from her healing and yet every bit as profound for me. After Carmen's healing, I never experienced any more problems with my own corneal ulcers! What an unexpected blessing for me!

Isn't the series of events interesting that led to Carmen and her need for help? I had brought with me to the Philippines the exact medication that Carmen would need. God used my medication to heal her. He could have done it without any medication or without my being involved. But God had allowed me to share in her healing. That incident with Carmen has had a profound effect upon my own faith life, my prayer life, and my daily walk with God.

Another observation concerning Carmen's situation was this: God will go to any length to accomplish His purpose for one of His children! It does not matter who they are or where they live. Also, simple life experiences (such as being a mom or handy with BAND- AIDS, etc.) are never wasted in God's economy! But what God does need is an obedient person, willing to travel halfway around the world to deliver the perfect medication. And that medication He would use to cure the eye problems of another child of His. Isn't it precious to know and love this kind of God who is so committed to us and to all of our needs? He is truly an awesome God!

Ginger and Carmen doing laundry

Galatians 6:2 (NKJV)

"Carry each other's burdens and in this way you will fulfill the law of Christ."

A footnote regarding Carmen's healing: The village chief's wife, a devout animist, came to me with her eye problems. She thought I could cure her as well. But after I looked at her eyes, I realized that she had cataracts. I knew that I could not help her. I grieved that there was nothing at all that I could do to help her regain her sight. I did suggest that she travel to Manila (nine hours away by bus) for help, but she sadly shook her head and walked away.

CHAPTER 21
The Bog

It was one of those hot, humid, sultry days. The sun beat down upon us mercilessly. Les and I had gone to Bagabag, our northern WBT center. Our reason for being there was to wash and dry our laundry and to purchase a few grocery supplies. Because of the extra humidity from three typhoons within a six- week period, we had a problem getting our clothes dry. Our wet jeans had mildewed hanging inside our nipa hut.

After finishing the laundry and shopping, we filled our backpacks with clean socks, underwear, sheets and our only blanket. But now we had another consideration—how we might carry the few grocery supplies we had purchased in addition to the laundry. Tough decisions needed to be made in order to maximize the available space required by those things based on their importance to us. First and foremost, of course, was the laundry.

Since our sheet-blanket was the only one we owned, it had to go into the backpack along with rest of our laundry. The problem was that these items were bulky and took up a lot of our very limited space.

Somehow we had to find space for the food items I had purchased. Whether to take the potatoes or not was a tough decision. Although they would add variety to our usual rice diet, unfortunately the potatoes added too much weight for my already overloaded backpack. A lengthy discussion with Les about the potatoes resulted in our removing them from my backpack. It was a painful decision, but I knew Les was right considering our tough climb back up the mountain to Ilap. Les would have to carry more than he could comfortably carry. His heaviest item was the large can of kerosene. That was absolutely necessary because of our lantern AND our borrowed, two-burner stove! I added a small tin (thank God for tins) of crackers to the bag I would be hand carrying and our packing was finished.

Since it was almost lunchtime, we decided to have lunch at the Bagabag Guest House, which was always a treat. It was like getting to eat out for us. Margaret Rhoads, who manned the Guest House, always welcomed unannounced guests with a hug and a smile. That made it all the more difficult for us to leave that loving and comforting environment. But the time had come for us to leave. We took our bulky backpacks as well as our bundles and walked out of the Guest House down to the paved road. Our task was to catch some sort of conveyance back to the Ifugao province. Usually our wait was a long one. But suddenly, a big luxurious bus rolled to a stop. We boarded it and sank deep into its plush, velvety seats. How delightful to experience such comfort, but especially the air- conditioning. We savored those luxuries for almost an hour's ride up the mountains to the Ifugao province where we lived. It was difficult to enjoy because I fretted about having to leave the cool comfort of the bus. Our momentary pleasures came to an abrupt halt when the bus rolled to a stop; it was time to retrieve our backpacks and begin our climb up the mountain.

We gathered our backpacks and our bundles and started our climb to Ilap along the carabao trail and to the place we called home. By that time it was two o'clock and the sun was unforgiving as it bore down upon us. We walked a while in complete silence saving our strength for what lay ahead of us. The only noises were the sounds of our labored breathing and our over-sized rubber boots as we trudged and plodded up the mountain.

Both of us were feeling the effects of the heat. I don't think we expected that it would be quite that hot, but the air was heavy with humidity, making it difficult to breathe. Sweat was running off our faces in rivulets as it stung our eyes, causing even more discomfort.

There was a place on that carabao trail which would allow us to take a shortcut. It was there that Les and I stopped to discuss our options. He feared it would be too difficult a climb for me considering all that I carried. But I assured him that I could manage. We began to press on using the shortcut. The tough part about the shortcut was the hill we must climb; it was a real killer because it was the old "knee-in-the-chest" type of climb. On a normal day it would have been a tough climb, but it was more difficult that day because of the amount of things we carried in our hands and on our backs; it allowed for no mistakes. After struggling and straining as we scaled up that hill, we finally reached a more level terrain. You would have thought we had just climbed Mt. Everest by the smiles we had! We paused to chat a second and wipe the sweat from our faces when we noticed the level ground presented some surprises for us.

There was one little carabao bog we hadn't known about. The carabao are very much like pigs and do not have sweat glands. They must have a cool, boggy place to wallow in order to cool down their body temperatures. Most carabao are used as work animals in the rice fields, pulling plows and hauling loads to and from the rice paddies. They were a necessity to the farmers who worked their rice crops. In the Ifugao province, a person owning a number of carabao was considered wealthy.

We had SO much rain from the three typhoons that Les and I had worn rubber boots that day. Up to that point, other than their being hot, it had been a very wise choice. The other surprise for us was in finding the trail that went THROUGH the bog was filled with water. Les and I had not known that it was full, not just with water, but with oozy, slimy mud. There was no way to go around the bog because the jungle grew thick on both sides of it.

My brave Les volunteered to be the first to enter the muddy bog. His boots were knee- high and since we had no way of knowing how deep the bog was, Les went ahead.

Slowly, he slogged across to the other side. Then he told me where to place my feet so I wouldn't get stuck in the muck and mire. With both of my arms filled, along with my backpack, I needed to make it across without getting our food or our laundry muddy. I believe I was on my third step when suddenly my rubber boot got stuck in the muck. Since my body was already moving forward, I fell face down in the bog.

Les waded into the bog and retrieved me, along with my muddy cargo and sat me down on a log. I hate to admit it but I cried like a baby. He took out his big, red bandana hankie from his back pocket and tried to mop the oozing mud from my face. I was exhausted! I was hot and humiliated! AND I was disgusted with myself! I felt really dumb for having fallen over like a two-year-old toddler into the muck. I wanted to go home, right then! I wanted to take my ice-cold, spring-fed shower, wash the mud off me and DIE.

Ahhh, but the humiliation wasn't over yet! We had another twenty-minute walk to our place. And we must pass several villagers' homes along our way. I knew that I was a sight to behold because they pointed and laughed at me. They weren't being unkind; maybe we were entertainment for them. I thought, "At least they have a new topic for discussion around their fires tonight." But then, so did we! At long last, we made it to our nipa hut.

One of the benefits of living in Ilap was that we learned to take joy in the simplest of things: a long-awaited ice-cold shower from the spring; clean sheets; a warm, clean sheet-blanket for our bed; and being happy to have made it back to the top of the mountain once again! But I, in particular, was grateful for a loving, caring, compassionate husband. He willingly climbed our highest mountain, sloshed through the muddiest muck to save me, and told me I was beautiful with bog mud still dripping off my face. I didn't believe him, but I loved him for saying it.

Ecclesiastes 4:9-10 (NIV)

"Two are better than one, because they have good return for their work; if one falls down, his friend can help him up. But pity the man who falls and has no one to help him up!

CHAPTER 22
Look Who's Watching

Adapting to another culture requires many adjustments. It is always a test for anyone who is willing to be scrutinized.

Sometimes Les and I passed the test. At other times we were complete and utter flops! And there were times when we were aware of our faux pas; at other times, we weren't. Sometimes those who were aware of them were much too gracious to tell us. But we did need to learn to view ourselves from the Filipinos' point of view. It was always a challenge for us to see how we were perceived by them.

Growing up in America, I had been taught to be independent, self-motivated and self- sufficient. But we soon discovered that those same characteristics could appear to the Filipinos as being prideful, arrogant and even snobbish. I was appalled to learn that. There were things about myself that I had not known before moving to the Philippines. I became aware of them while living in Ilap. We were secluded from people of our own language and culture there. I discovered that I needed my own private space. My ability to move about unhampered and without being under the watchful eye of other people was important to me. Imagine trying to do that while living in a culture where your skin, hair color and ethnicity were obviously different. Being different is not always a plus. You might be surprised to discover that, just as I was.

Another thing I discovered was that I would NEVER have been able to be a celebrity for all the same reasons! Some people might be surprised to learn that there are a few of us who have NO desire to be famous! I found it to be rather silly, but interesting, to realize that about myself!

In Ilap we had an outside shower with no door! I learned very quickly that if I wanted to take a shower in private, it must be done while all the village children were still in school. When I wanted to take a shower, Les would hook up the bamboo pipes from the spring to our hut. Then I hurriedly took my shower and washed my hair. The water from the spring was as cold as refrigerated water. Its temperature was almost unbearable. I made Olympic time in getting my shower accomplished! One doesn't dilly-dally when taking an ice-cold shower, especially in the cooler mountain air.

One day, when I had THOUGHT all the kids were in school, I decided to shave my legs. After all, I was alone in our little nipa hut. Or so I thought. I sat down in the middle of the floor with a little container of water and began shaving my legs.

It's not clear exactly when I became aware that someone was watching me. But as I glanced up and out the door, there stood the two little brothers, Victor and Alex. They were watching me transfixed. Neither of them, I'm absolutely sure, had ever seen a lady shave her legs, much less a puti-puti (POO tee-POO tee), a very white lady! Both of the boys had backed up as far as they could without falling off into the ravine behind them. Of course, they wanted to get a better view. And that was no small task since our hut was six feet off the ground on poles. I had to laugh too since they were both in hysterics, pointing at me and giggling.

That was the day I became convinced that being a celebrity, or being watched and admired, was certainly not for me. As an American, I liked my space. And I most certainly did not need the attention of two grinning, gawking, giggling brothers. I wanted privacy for whatever chore I needed to do. Being the center of attention was definitely not for me!

Matthew 6:34

"Do not be anxious for tomorrow; for tomorrow will care for itself. Each day has enough trouble of its own."

CHAPTER 23
Under the Circumstances

Our FTC time was the most stretching times in our lives for Les and me. Everything was new: the Ifugao culture, language, the food and their habits. We felt a kinship to the biblical disciples because, like them, there were 12 of us as well. We came from all walks of life and like the original 12 disciples, some even knew how to fish. There were nurses and other professionals from the corporate world, as well as pastors and college students, in the group. Les was an engineer and I was a wife, mother, and grandmother. But God had brought all of us to that particular time and place to learn how to be Bible translators, literacy workers and language learners. The particular goal for Les and me was to make it through our training course with grace and dignity. We did NOT want to bring shame upon our new trainee friends, our organization, or especially, upon the Lord. We wanted to do our VERY BEST under the circumstances.

I learned that "under the circumstances" covered a lot of areas of our lives. One of our circumstances was that we had outdoor plumbing. Actually, there was no plumbing—just the great outdoors! But after about three weeks we graduated to three bamboo walls.

There wasn't even a DOOR to close for privacy. We had no roof over our comfort room (C.R.) either. Our C.R. was what Americans would commonly call an "outhouse." Our friend and neighbor Paterno had built the C.R. for us. He was kind enough to make it face the big ravine in back of our nipa hut. Paterno, along with his son Leon, had dug a huge pit and then set the bamboo walls over a wooden plank floor. In the middle of that floor he had cut a square hole. And THAT was our C.R. We were told it was one of the nicest ones in all the Ilap area. I took their word for it. I was not about to check out the other C.R.s. Since our C.R. didn't have a roof, we had to use our huge yellow and orange National Airlines umbrella when it rained (and it rained all the time). It fit perfectly over the top of the bamboo walls and kept us dry while using the facilities.

In the evening when it was time to go to bed, there were things that must be done in preparation for sleeping. One of them was to set up our mosquito netting. THAT was a test of our ingenuity, patience, spirituality and character. But it most certainly required more ingenuity than either of us could muster at that time of the evening! Les had devised a particular plan for setting up the mosquito netting. The netting had loops on each of the four corners. Then two bamboo poles, similar to fishing poles, needed to be threaded through the loops. Afterwards, Les ran a rope up and over the ceiling beam of the hut and down to the opposite end of the pole. With that side done, it was necessary to repeat the process for the remaining end. After completing that nightly task, we were both exhausted. The last thing we needed to do was to tuck in the netting around the four-inch foam mattress that lay on the floor. And that was what we optimistically called our bed. It was an "iffy thing" whether or not we were still speaking to each other after assembling the mosquito netting. Our nightly exercise was character- building and flaw- revealing. Just as an onion has some unwanted layers, God had begun to peel away the unwanted layers of our lives. And God was using nylon netting to do it! Peeling away some layers was painful; for others, it was comical.

One night, after setting up the mosquito netting, we settled down to pray together. That was our usual routine. It was a good routine. By that time both of us had a lot of confessing to do about our attitudes and impatience with each other. The assembling of the mosquito netting became our nightly testing time. Lying there in the dark we prayed together. We learned to focus on praises toward God for how wonderful He continued to be to us. His blessings of safety, His provisions and care were some of the praises we shared with Him. It was a great way to end our day under any circumstance.

With the mosquito netting securely and tightly tucked in all around our mattress, I reasoned that NOTHING could touch me. However, we were aware of several varieties of varmints in our nipa hut. We could hear the rats jumping off the beams overhead and onto the floor. But I told myself that as long as I had that mosquito netting tucked in tightly around me, I was safe! I can't imagine what I was thinking! Rats there were known to eat Tupper Ware containers as if they were potato chips! Surely the flimsy, nylon mosquito netting could be devoured as if it were a snack as well!

Despite ALL the work we had just done to secure the mosquito netting around our mattress, it was not uncommon for me to realize that I needed to visit our C. R. Les always groaned when I informed him of my decision to get up and out of the netting! But on this particular night, I grabbed my flashlight only to discover that the batteries were dead. "Oh, well," I thought, "Who needs a flashlight? I know my way to the C. R." I opened our bamboo door, put our ladder down and backed down the ladder (there IS a right and wrong way to ascend or descend a ladder). By that time I was hurrying to get to the C. R. at breakneck speed.

The night was as black as pitch with no moonlight whatsoever—a total blackout! Suddenly, I ran smack into something huge, hairy and immovable! I hit the beast so hard that I literally bounced off the unknown creature. Yet it still stood solidly and firmly in my way. The horrible thing was that I KNEW it was alive and breathing; I could hear it and feel its warm body next to me.

I yelled for Les, who always came to my rescue. Les managed a fast exit from the hut with his flashlight in hand and then he started laughing. I had run headlong into Paterno's carabao. Carabao are grayish-black, just like the night. Because there was no light, not even moonlight on that night, I had no way of seeing that huge, black, hulk of an animal. Before that moment we had never known that Paterno had kept his carabao underneath our hut at night. Since our hut was six feet off the ground and set on poles, evidently it was the perfect place to store a carabao.

The carabao was benignly unaware that it had almost scared the life out of me. Under the circumstances, I had even forgotten my purpose for being out there in the middle of the night. I just stood and stared at the big, black carabao and was grateful that I had not run into its horns.

Psalm 31:15 (NKJV)

"My times are in Your hands."

CHAPTER 24
The Two Brothers

Victor and Alex were Ilap boys. They were two of the nine children in their family. Victor was about seven years old and Alex was around five. The reason their ages were ambiguous is that they really don't know their actual birth date. Births are usually remembered by events such as, "the year of the big storm" or "the year of the bad flood." Victor and Alex's mom was a widow and a very sweet Christian lady. They lived close enough for us to hear her singing hymns with her children at night, but we were not able to see their house because of the trees and bushes.

    Victor, I was told, had polio when he was very small. That left him with a limp when he walked. Also, he had stiffness in one of his hands. But that hand didn't stop Victor from being a normal kid who was able to do almost anything except to attend the little one- room schoolhouse for his lessons. His mom had told Victor and Alex that their job was to care for the carabao. Carabao are huge and have horns along with a very nasty temper. But Alex and Victor led that huge, hunk of a hostile animal around like a puppy dog on a string! Because I was from Texas, I was impressed with those two little cowboys.

Because our nipa hut was six feet off the ground and on poles, we used the space below the hut as an outdoor room. There was a table beneath it with places for people to sit. The kids (mainly Alex and Victor) would play beneath our house during the day while the other children were still in school. Quite honestly, neither Les nor I minded the boys' being there. They did bring life to our rather uneventful lives with their giggles and chatter in their Ayangan language. And because Les and I were supposed to learn their language, we enjoyed the children for two other reasons: 1) children speak more slowly and use simpler words and sentence structure, and 2) children are not ashamed to correct language mistakes. Most adults were too shy to do that. For Les and me, it was a win-win situation!

One day as I sat below the house studying language, I saw Alex and Victor running down the carabao path on the hill just above us; I knew they were coming to see us. I had some paper and pencils and both boys stood and watched me write down some words. I could tell that they REALLY wanted to write using the pencils and paper. Even owning paper and pencils was uncommon for them. I gave a pencil to Victor and I watched as he carefully and painstakingly wrote his name. But after I had passed the pencil to Alex, he looked at me with wistful eyes and my heart broke for him. I knew that he did not know how to write his name. I took the pencil from Alex and wrote the ABCs across the top of the page. Then I showed Alex that his name was a part of the ABCs. I could see in his eyes that he understood the concept. Next, I wrote Alex's name in large letters. Then I had Alex take his pencil and go over the letters that I had written. He was able to copy the letters though I could see him struggle due to his lack of fine motor skills. But Alex was determined. I could tell that by the way his tongue poked out the corner of his mouth as if that could help him write the difficult, curved letters. Afterwards, I had Alex write his name without my help and with nothing to copy. He did fine.

Every day, at about one o'clock, Victor and Alex would come and sit under our hut and we worked together on their ABCs and numbers. We also counted aloud. The two little boys were as happy as they could be. It was a pleasure seeing how much they loved learning and watching them progress daily.

A couple of weeks later Les said to me, "I see Alex coming down the hill." Yes, I too could see him as he made his way toward our hut. He had that determined look on his face like "a little man on a mission." Alex was carrying something behind his back as he shyly approached our hut. Using only one hand, Alex very carefully climbed the ladder to our hut. He plopped down a large bunch of bananas in our doorway. I got up to thank him but he just giggled and scampered away. I was glad that he did because I had a lump in my throat that was the size of Texas. I knew that little boy was very poor (money-wise). But Alex had wanted to repay me. The bananas were his gift to show me that he appreciated my helping him learn to write his name. I was deeply touched. How does one show love? Sometimes, it's with bananas!

Psalm 127:3

"Behold, children are a gift of the Lord."

CHAPTER 25
Three Words You Never Want To Hear

There are several things that a person would need to know if he/she intended to live in a nipa hut. To me the first and most important one becomes apparent after dark.

A person would need to know that lighting a lantern inside the hut allows anyone outside to see through the bamboo walls; they become virtually transparent. I was reminded of an old movie I saw starring Clark Gable and Ava Gardner. The movie was called Mogambo. One particular scene shows Ava Gardner going into her tent where she begins to undress. At that point, only ONE thing kept that movie from being "R-rated." Just as she was about to undress, a lion strolled through her tent; she froze as she watched in mortal fear! For some reason, that scene has been burned into my mind forever. Maybe it's because I had lived in Africa and I already knew that living in the jungle presented problems of its own; things just don't stay PUT at night!

Les and Ginger by the ladder leading into their nipa hut

I've had some experience with living in a nipa hut during our training in the Philippines. Our nipa hut was blackened by smoke from cooking inside. Daily we opened our four doors to allow sunlight inside. The two peaks of our nipa hut (at each roof end) were open and I'm sure the original plan was for airflow. But the bats, rats and other things that "go bump in the night" had no way of knowing that they were not invited to enter our hut. By *Ifugao standards, our* hut was very nice. By American standards with no running water, no toilet, no electricity and no windows, it would have been condemned! But we were missionaries in training.

We had two pieces of furniture; both of them Les had thoughtfully made for me. My furniture looked similar to something Tarzan and Jane might have had; they were very roughly made. One of the pieces of furniture was similar to a coffee table. And that is where we ate our meals as we sat Indian-style or cross- legged on the floor. The other piece of furniture looked more like a bookcase.

It was used for storing tins of oatmeal, flour, salt, crackers and oil. I used it as my pantry.

Our dishes, cups, forks and knives (we had only two of each) were kept in drawstring bags and those hung from nails on the walls. Putting the utensils in drawstring bags helped to keep varmints away from them. We had only one sharp knife and it was Les' buck knife; we ARE from Texas. It was inconvenient for me if he happened to be gone when I needed his knife. After washing the dishes, I poured boiling water over them using a dish drainer that I had set over a large aluminum pan. My hope was that it would kill some of the germs. After they dried, I put them back in the drawstring bags and hung the bags on the nails.

Writing letters to our family, friends and the people who financially supported us was one responsibility I enjoyed. I did all of mine at night. It became my time to sit and think about the activities of our day; I shared those in our letters. One night, I had gotten all of my writing paraphernalia out to write letters. I sat on our mattress in the middle of the floor. But after a time, I became tired with nothing to lean back on. Les helped me to maneuver the mattress over close to a wall. There I could lean back on one of the supporting posts of the hut. It was much more comfortable that way. I continued writing letters. Les was sitting a few feet away at our table using our little red lantern to read his Bible. But lantern light is such a poor excuse for lighting! I could have lit a match and gotten about the same wattage! Because of the black ceiling and walls, we weren't able to see much of anything using just our lantern for light. But Les did see something!

Suddenly, he turned to me and said, "Honey, don't move!" Those were words you never wanted to hear! What would be the first thing you wanted to do if someone said those words to you? I wanted to run screaming into the night! But like a dutiful wife, I sat perfectly still. Les came toward me with a piece of firewood and smacked the biggest spider I'd ever seen! SHE was no ordinary spider! She was a very pregnant spider carrying a kazillion *babies in* a sac. When Les hit her, the babies sprayed ALL over our bed and me. Our bed looked as if it had black pepper on it—except that the "pepper" had legs and baby spiders were running EVERYWHERE! I jumped up and ran for a can of bug spray. I sprayed our bed, thoroughly saturating the blanket that I had sat on. We took the blanket and dumped the baby spiders out our door. Les assured me that all of the spiders were dead.

When we went to bed, we HAD to use that blanket for cover; it was the ONLY one we had. But the blanket "squeaked" every time we moved in bed. I know it sounds ridiculous, but it was true! However, the smell of the bug spray we used was more offensive than either of us could bear! We took the blanket off and spent a cold and miserable night huddling together trying to keep warm. The nights were cold up in the mountains. High on our *agenda the* following morning was laundering that blanket!

These are only a few of the things that a person would need to know before living in a nipa hut.

Proverbs 24:10 (NIV)

"If you falter in times of trouble, how small is your strength."

CHAPTER 26
Visiting Sparrows

When Les and I were living in Ifugao, the entire country began to experience a great deal of civil unrest. However, Les and I felt reasonably safe because we didn't see ourselves as a threat to anyone. We had no political axe to grind. After all, we had been sent to Ilap for training with the national Bible translation group.

The ordinary daily tasks in Ilap required a lot from us. The only "running water" I had was Les running to and from the spring carrying water in long, hollowed-out bamboo tubes. There was not a single timesaving device in our lives like we had back home! Home for us had been four bedrooms, two baths, two living areas, two dining areas, a dishwasher, hot and cold running water, a refrigerator, a laundry room with a Maytag washer and dryer. It was not even close to being like home! But we had understood that when we accepted the challenge of training in Ilap.

In addition to our normal tasks, we had assignments for our language training as well. We were to ask particular questions of our Ifugao friends and record their answers using a tape recorder for proper pronunciation. The lessons were designed to hone our skills and help us learn the Ayangan language. It was necessary for us to record the information in a daily log also. Then Nel Binayao, the head of our field training group, could assess our progress.

On the last afternoon before Les and I were to leave Ilap, we had noticed that our nearby next-door neighbor Paterno had visitors. He came over and climbed up our ladder to talk with us. I smiled and said to him, "Paterno, I see that you have visitors today." He smiled and nodded. Then I said to him, "Are they your family?" Paterno shook his head and said, "No." Being one who never gave up until I got answers, I asked, "Oh, then they are your friends?" Again Paterno shook his head and said, "No, no friends." I thought to myself, "Not family, not friends; who could they be then?" Paterno said to me, "They are looking for antiques." I laughed. Antiques? People up in Ilap hardly had anything, but antiques were out of the question!

Paterno left and I was busily packing things for our departure early the next morning. I happened to look out my door and noticed that one of the "antique" guys was sitting on Paterno's rock fence, which faced our hut. He was reading a newspaper. At least he wanted us to think that he was reading a newspaper! When I would glance away, he would drop the paper down a little so he could watch me. It was very disturbing. In a comical way it was like watching an old, but very bad, detective movie. The <u>Pink Panther</u> with Peter Sellers popped into my mind. Just then Les came in from his chores and asked me, "Who's the guy watching our hut?" I told him, "An antique dealer." Then Les laughed, too. "Hmm," I thought, "that made me feel safer!"

Another "antique dealer" arrived and boldly stared into our hut, watching our every move. By that time, it was almost dark outside. A sense of foreboding began to creep into my mind with the visitors so blatantly watching our every move. Les and I tried to carry on our packing tasks in a normal way. But it was not easy while knowing that we were being spied upon. Surprisingly, both of us slept well when we went to bed later that night.

Very early the next morning we left Ilap to rendezvous with our trainee teammates at the bottom of the mountain. When all the trainees arrived, we were loaded into vans to return to the Wycliffe Center in Bagabag. Our four-month assignment in Ilap had been completed. As our group members arrived one by one, they carried all their training gear with them. Each of them reported a similar experience with the two "visitors." We learned that we had been checked out by men known as "Sparrows," members of the "New Peoples' Army." Even though the Sparrows were a small communist gorilla group, they had networks all over the Philippine Islands. Recently they had moved into the remote areas such as Ilap. The New Peoples' Army had a bad reputation for their method of dealing with unwanted people. As it happened though, we were leaving and it seemed just at the right time. I suspect that Les and I had been the last people on their visitation list. I've always heard that "timing is everything." We were more than persuaded of that now.

Our training/living in Ilap did provide many benefits for Les and me. Learning to live in circumstances beyond what would be called normal for us helped us to see:

1. *God's protection, His mercies, His love and His powerful presence with us daily.*

2. *The incredible ways God chose to help us in our times of need were always a surprise to us. Rarely did He answer our prayers as we had expected, but He did answer them.*
3. *Why His name is called "Faithful and True;" we were able to see and experience that about Him.*
4. *His powerful presence in our lives. THAT both awed and encouraged us.*

Les and I will forever treasure the memories of those times when He quietly came to our rescue. There were no bells or whistles or any big "tah-dahs." There was only the quiet, comfortable peace of His presence.

Psalm 77:11

"I shall remember the deeds of the Lord; surely I will remember Thy wonders of old. I will meditate on all Thy work, and muse on Thy deeds. Thy way, O God, is holy; what god is like our God?"

Part 4—Life After Ilap

It was a nine-hour bus ride from Ilap to Manila. Our new jobs in Manila were already awaiting us. Physically we had left Ilap, but emotionally our ties there were still strong. But now it was time to "switch hats" from our FTC roles to our new roles and responsibilities in Manila. However, we had only the bus ride back to Manila to try to re-acclimate ourselves for the tasks that lay before us.

The jobs for which Les would be responsible were the entire Manila center with its many facets. That meant he would be over the Guest House (basically a small hotel with 21 rooms), the office and national staff members, the shop, the grounds of the center, etc. I don't know how he was able to do so many things but I'm sure it had a lot to do with his organizational skills. I was one Director Dave Ohlson's assistant. My job had many variations, but most of the time I worked on special projects for him. Later on, when a pressing need arose for a travel agent for our organization, I was asked to fill that need also. Many of our translators flew to other countries all over the world to present papers at universities. They spoke on linguistics, anthropology and a host of other topics. Because of the international travel needs, the job also required me to be responsible for passports, visas and compliance with immigration regulations. I loved my job, especially making travel arrangements and getting the best possible deals for our people.

Finding suitable housing for us in Manila was our first big project. We needed to be accessible to public transportation; we did not have a car at that time. We found an apartment within walking distance of our Manila center. Things for us began to feel more normal once we found our own place to live. We enjoyed everything in Manila but the traffic; it was a colossal mess. With 12 million people trying to cross the streets wherever they could, there are no words to describe the hazards this presented for the people who drove. Sometimes it was funny, but at other times it was alarming.

With our own apartment and jobs to do, we felt at peace and more at home in the new place where God had called us to serve. There is nothing on this planet more satisfying than knowing you are exactly where God wants you. That is the way both Les and I felt about our being with WBT/SIL in Manila.

CHAPTER 27
The Best Sore Throat I Ever Had

I'm a Texas gal and, like most Texans, we LOVE iced tea. I was bemoaning the fact that, due to a really bad sore throat, the doctor would not allow me to drink iced or cold beverages. He insisted that I drink only HOT tea. Drinking hot tea in the States is a wonderful experience, especially in the fall and winter. But now we lived in Manila, where the heat and humidity matched no other city in which I've ever lived. Consequently, I would just suffer and drink my hot tea.

I was sipping my hot tea and wearing a sweatband when I heard Les and our Filipina helper Elma laughing. I thought I had better go to the kitchen and check out their hilarity. There they stood peering into our dark green, glass pitcher. Elma was saying to Les, "But Sir, I don't know how it happened. I had even put plastic wrap over this pitcher!" Then Elma pointed into the pitcher and slowly backed away so that I could peer into it as well. On the bottom of the pitcher lay the lifeless, limp body of some little creature. "My goodness, Elma, what is that?" I asked.

I had thought and maybe even hoped that she would give me the Tagalog word for the little creature. Both Les and I were in language school learning the Tagalog language. As a matter of fact, I knew what the creature was; it was a gecko! With her dark eyes flashing like "a deer in the headlights," Elma looked up at me and said, "Lee-zard." Hearing her answer, I convulsed with laughter. I was reminded of the verse:

Proverbs 17:22

"A joyful heart is good medicine..."

For the past week I had been the one who had griped about having to drink tepid water and hot tea! Peering into the pitcher, I saw the lifeless lizard lying on the bottom. And then I noticed something else; the lizard's tail was missing! Neither Les nor Elma had noticed that. Where, I wondered, was that lizard's tail? I dared not think too long about what could have happened to it! But I had to admit I was smiling over some of the possibilities!

In spite of the missing tail, I had not noticed any visible or unusual differences in Les' behavior, such as running up walls and hanging from the ceiling. Regrettably, the end of the tail was never discovered. But I have developed a greater appreciation for hot tea, even there in the sweltering Philippine heat. I'm still laughing over the tailless lizard incident!

Proverbs 15:13

"A joyful heart makes a cheerful face."

CHAPTER 28
The Best Sermon I Ever Saw

One day as I visited the CRIBS (Creating Responsive Infants By Serving) orphanage, three little sisters were brought in. Joanne was the oldest at age five. Her sister Jinko was four and Baby Jasmine was only 18 months old. They had been brought to CRIBS before, but eventually their mother came back for them and took them home. Once again she left them, but it was permanent this time. That made them available for adoption. I never learned why the mother could no longer take care of her daughters. It must have been heartbreaking for her to give up her three beautiful daughters.

Baby Jasmine was hysterical. I have never witnessed such emotional trauma by a child that young! Jasmine cried uncontrollably with deep, dry sobs. Sweat poured from her entire body. A pool of perspiration lay on the mat where she sat. Joanne and Jinko sat numbly by Jasmine; both of them stared off into space with empty eyes. Also sitting on the mat was three-year-old Josephine; she had watched the entire, tragic scene unfold. Tiny little Josephine never said a word, but crawled over and sat behind Jasmine. Then Josephine began patting Jasmine on her back. She continued to pat Jasmine; thump-pause, thump-pause, thump-pause for more than half an hour. Jasmine eventually fell asleep on the floor from sheer exhaustion. However, she continued to sob, even in her sleep.

That day I witnessed the best sermon I had ever seen! I saw *profound* mercy, grace and loving compassion, all demonstrated by three-year-old Josephine. I can never erase that vision of compassion, nor will I ever forget Josephine or Jasmine. On that awful but beautiful day, I witnessed something so special and rare that even remembering that scene brings tears to my eyes. Josephine comforted one little brokenhearted Baby Jasmine.

I asked the nurse Tina Tan about Josephine and what we had just witnessed. Tina said to me, "Josephine knew exactly what to do because, only three weeks ago, her own mother had brought her to CRIBS and left her."

Josephine had understood the awfulness and rawness of Jasmine's pain through her own personal experience. She knew how Jasmine felt. She knew that what Jasmine needed was not words, but an expression of love. And it was done in a way that only Baby Jasmine could understand—a 'thump' of love from a kindred spirit.

Corinthians 13:4

"Love is patient, love is kind..."

Jinko, Josephine, and Joanne holding baby William

CHAPTER 29
The Adoption

Neither Les nor I could have dreamed in 1988 that we would even consider being parents again! Both of our grown children were married and had children of their own. But something began to happen to us that involved an orphanage and a little girl there. This is the story of how this twentieth-century "Abraham and Sarah" were confronted with that prospect. My intention in sharing this story is to show God's faithfulness to us as we experienced dramatic life changes in the days and months that followed.

It all began quite innocently. After many urgings from my missionary girlfriends, I began to frequent an orphanage called CRIBS close to our WBT/SIL offices. Initially, I began visiting CRIBS once a week, but I quickly learned that there were too many babies and not enough help there. Each baby needed to be hugged, fed, changed or rocked. After seeing their desperate needs, I decided to go to CRIBS twice a week.

During my first visit to CRIBS, I was confronted with such colossal needs there that it staggered and overwhelmed me. I walked to one of the large, screened windows in the playroom area and tears rolled down my face. I remember saying to God, "Okay, this is Your one and only opportunity to have me here. I do not ever plan to return! Whatever it is that I need to know, learn, or discover, You need to show me." The Lord wasted no time in rebuking my heart. Quietly He spoke to my heart and said, "You think you are having a difficult time here? You can leave any time you want! These children have no place to go. You are My hands and feet. I want you to show My love to these babies. Unless you come here to feed, hug and rock them, who will do it?" After that time, I began going there several times a week. Working only half days in my job with the mission allowed me time to volunteer at CRIBS. They really needed help.

The orphanage was in a very large, old-fashioned, two-story house. Their administrative offices were downstairs, along with their laundry facilities. All of the rooms upstairs were where the babies were kept. A large sala, Spanish for living area, was their playroom. The older children played on two large mats on the floor. Rocking chairs, toys and games were kept there in that area for the children. In front of the sala was a covered stairway that led from the parking area upstairs to the playroom. At the top of the stairway was an expandable steel gate to keep the toddlers safely upstairs. Most of the babies were three months to three years old. Those younger babies lay on the mats and played with little hand-held toys. Though too young to participate with the older children, the younger babies loved watching their activities and antics.

The newborns and other infants, though, were kept away from the older babies. Their room was the smallest of all the rooms. It had only six or seven cribs for the newborns. An adjacent bedroom held cribs for babies three months to one-year-old. The last bedroom, across on the opposite side of the sala, was for children over one-year-old. All three bedrooms had cribs that lined the perimeter of the walls. In addition, more cribs were placed down the center of each bedroom. The rooms were completely filled with cribs. That orphanage had room for only 35 babies and it stayed full most of the time. When one child left CRIBS, another child took his/her place.

The upstairs section had a kitchen where food and formula were prepared for all of the children. One other room was used as an isolation room for any baby suspected of having anything contagious.

Interested people and donations funded CRIBS orphanage; it was not state-funded. But the Department of Social Welfare and Development (DSWD) supervised it. No doctor was on staff there, but there were two very capable nurses who worked 12- hour shifts. One of them was Tina Tan who had worked in the huge and well-known medical center in Houston, Texas. She was wonderful with the babies and almost as good as a doctor in caring for them. Some U.S. Embassy wives came and helped care for the children weekly. CRIBS was not the perfect place for orphaned children, but it was a good and safe place. With limited funds and resources, godly people ran the orphanage and did their best to provide good care for the children. However, it was the volunteers like myself who came and helped care for the children's needs on a more regular basis. Feeding time was a hectic and critical time as we tried to feed each child as quickly as possible.

On my first visit to CRIBS, I took one of the babies in my arms to rock him. Instantly, there were six other children "attached" to me on every visible piece of my flesh. There were three in my lap and one on either side of the rocker "hanging on" and a child on the back of the rocker hugging my neck. I decided to sing to them. I'm not a singer, but they didn't seem to mind. I sang, "Jesus Loves Me" to them. I wanted them to hear about Jesus from me. That day I sang and cried as I rocked them; their needs were so palpable. One April day as I sat on one of the large floor mats, two new baby girls arrived, each about three months old. One looked very Chinese and I learned that she was brought to CRIBS because she would be fed well. She would be leaving to meet her new family in Australia soon. Both baby girls had health issues. They were underweight and had huge, ugly, oozing boils on their heads. Someone had shaved the hair from one of the little girls' head on both sides. That left a narrow strip of hair down the middle of her head. She looked to me like a little "Mohawk" Indian baby. Tiny turquoise earrings dotted her ears. When baby girls are born in the Philippines, their ears are pierced and earrings inserted. That made it easy for me to distinguish baby girls from baby boys in the orphanage.

The Mohawk baby stared intently at me; she had huge black eyes. Whenever she saw me, she followed me with her eyes. Because of the inflamed and oozing boils on both girls' heads, my initial response was to walk away from them. I didn't want to touch them! But again, the Lord spoke to my heart and said, "You with your sensitive heart—if you walk away, who will ever hold these two babies or show love to them?" I began to hold them and care for their needs. But despite all my efforts to keep from being contaminated by their disease, similar painful boils appeared on both my arms.

My good friend Lily Torrente said to me, "Ginger, you need to go see my cousin in Cubao (coo BOUGH)! He's a dermatologist; he can help you." Quickly, I made an appointment with him. He immediately asked me, "Where have you been?" I replied, "Tell me what I have and I'll tell you where I've been." The doctor said, "You have a type of viral infection." Then he told me that the infection that both baby girls had was due to their lack of care in the other holding facility before coming to CRIBS. Lily's cousin gave me prescriptions for the babies and myself. Quickly, the three of us healed using the medicine for our viral infections.

One day I said to Les, "You know, these children have a very warped sense of family. They see only women in the orphanage. Would you be willing to come on your coffee break and let the children see you?" He agreed to do that. Afterwards, Les began to spend time at CRIBS. The little Mohawk baby girl was particularly interested in Les. I laughed and teased Les telling him, "She's starting very young in knowing how to woo a guy." But Les spent time holding her and talking to her; she was fascinated with him. By that time the little Mohawk baby with no first name was five months old and she rarely ever cried. Les and "Baby Girl Fernandez," as she was known there, began to feel very comfortable with each other. After a time though, it became necessary for Les to rock her to sleep so that he could return to work. She wouldn't cry, but her chin would quiver when he tried to lay her down in bed. Les hated to leave her unless she was asleep, but she tried hard not to go to sleep. That became the routine for Les' time with Baby Girl Fernandez in the beginning of their relationship.

Les with "Hannah" at CRIBS

The nurse Tina told me that she had decided to give Baby Girl Fernandez a first name. She said, "I wanted to give her a strong Christian name." Tina named her "Hannah." The Hebrew translation of the name Hannah is grace or mercy. We liked the name Hannah and we were pleased with Tina's choice for her. But it was a strange coincidence to me because it had been one of my grandmother's names.

At this point in Philippine history, President Ferdinand Marcos' rule was characterized by political unrest and rampant corruption. That resulted in his being deposed. The new president Corrie Aquino took charge through something called "The Peaceful Revolution." We were pleased with the new president, but that change in power meant a new head for the DSWD.

The newly appointed woman decided to make changes within the department by revising the adoption laws. A full-page ad was published in all of the newspapers in Manila stating that the adoption law was about to change in August.

Another new situation arose that became a problem for us, too. The newly formed Philippine government decided not to renew the contracts for the two U.S. military bases, Clark and Subic. Shortly after that happened, Les and I felt God leading us to adopt baby Hannah. Two attorney friends, Caesar Ramirez and his wife Vicki, were in a small group with us called "Koinonia." In the beginning, it met most of the time in our home. Vicki and Caesar agreed to legally take on the DSWD, especially the country's newly formed adoption laws. The new law stated that no foreigner while residing in the Philippines would be allowed to adopt there. The hopeful parents would need to return to their home country and set up residence there for two years before applying for adoption. Only after complying with these new requirements would they be considered as adoptive parents. For Les and me, the new law didn't make sense! If we were living in the Philippines, the DSWD would be able to monitor us, interview us, do their "home studies," do background checks, and check on a host of other requirements.

In July and just weeks before the August deadline, Les and I went to the DSWD. We asked them for adoption papers for Hannah, but they denied our request. Their reason was that the law was going to change. We said, "Yes, we understand. That is why we came now because we know the law is going to change." We went on to say, "But the new law does not go into effect for several more days; we are still under the old law." Yet they would not provide the necessary paperwork for us. Two weeks later we were notified both personally and in the newspapers that the new law had been made retroactive; it now included us. Our attorneys filed our lawsuit emphasizing the statement in their new law that declared, "…All actions taken must be in the best interest of the child."

My birthday is in October and since I was a regular at the orphanage, the workers at CRIBS decided to give me a present for my birthday. They allowed Les and me to have Hannah for the weekend. We were ecstatic and delighted to have the 10-month-old Hannah with us. We signed her out for the weekend on Friday and returned her on Monday morning as prearranged. After returning Hannah to CRIBS that Monday, I left for work at our mission office. But the non-crying Hannah cried and cried. At noon, CRIBS called and asked me to come and take Hannah home to live with us. However, there was a proviso that Les and I would agree to return Hannah to CRIBS if the DSWD needed to see her. And we agreed to do that. Three times we returned Hannah to the orphanage so that the DSWD could see her and know that she was being well cared for.

There were about 65 children who fell between the old adoption law and the new one. We had learned that 35 children had already been taken back from their adoptive parents by the DSWD. It grieved us to think that this could possibly happen to us. We had heard tragic stories of the DSWD going into the homes of adoptive parents at 10 o'clock at night to take back the children. Once we took Hannah, now renamed "Hannah-Joy," and hid out with her in the home of Ed and Page Cvelich, missionaries with the Navigators. They too were in our Koinonia group. The idea of someone trying to take her from us was unthinkable. It grieved our hearts to even consider such a possibility. We had a taste of that when we had respected the agreement and taken Hannah-Joy back to CRIBS for the DSWD to see her. We had complied with their requests on three previous occasions. But on the fourth and last time that we returned her, she began to shake all over when we stepped out of the car at CRIBS. By that time, Hannah-Joy was walking, talking and being a typical 15-month-old child. That day, we put her back in the car and left. It was apparent that she loved us and we loved her; we were bonded to one another. Our concerns were that the DSWD would remove Hannah-Joy from our loving care, move her to some other holding place or orphanage, and we would never see her again. It was a heavy burden for us to bear. The new adoption law stating that whatever is done must be in the best interest of the child puzzled us. How was it possible to take a baby from two loving parents in a stable environment, only to place her back into an institution? How could that possibly be in her best interest? She had been ABANDONED! There were NO birth parents waiting in the balcony for her.

At that time, there were many people all over the world who were praying for our situation and us. One morning in early March 1990, 19 months after applying to adopt Hannah-Joy, I read in my daily devotion this Scripture:

Isaiah 61:1-2 (NIV)

*"He has sent me to bind up the brokenhearted,
to proclaim freedom for the captives and
release from darkness for the prisoners, to
proclaim the year of the Lord's favor..."*

For reasons I couldn't explain, those words seemed to be meant for us. "Yes," I thought, "we were brokenhearted, prisoners of the adoption law and I was ready to 'proclaim the year of the Lord's favor' for us." That morning as I read those words, it was as if the words were highlighted; they grabbed my attention. Nothing in our adoption woes had changed to my knowledge, but God had used the Isaiah 61 verses to give my heart hope. A little while later when I went to our mailbox, we had received a letter from *Shirle Smith*, one of our friends and supporters in Friendswood, Texas. Shirle had written her letter to us 12 days earlier. She wrote us, "I have a verse for you that the Lord gave to me. *It is Isaiah 61:1-2!*" They were the exact words the Lord had shown me earlier that morning during my devotional time. How great is our God to bring us hope in our seemingly hopeless situation! It was if God were saying to us, "The end is in sight! Hold on and don't give up or waiver in your faith."

Many people tried to help us legally find solutions to the horrendous problems faced in our pursuit of adopting children like Hannah-Joy. One of the Philippines' retired Chief Justices of the Supreme Court, Chief Justice Alampay

(AL lum pie), worked tirelessly on our behalf. He was a remarkable born-again Christian who had a passion for justice and he knew their laws well. But there were others (well-meaning friends/acquaintances) who also knew about our struggles in adoption and offered us illegal ways to leave the country. We had been, as Scripture says, "tested by fire" for almost 19 months PAST our furlough time. I want to admit now, for just a moment, we were tempted to do that because we wanted the pain to stop! The testing of our faith was so stretching that I feared we would break or do something to disappoint God. The book of James says, "… persevering in troubles produces patience." God most certainly wanted us to wait patiently for HIM to lead us through the trials of our adoption of Hannah-Joy.

Psalm 66:10, 12 (NIV)

"For you, O God, tested us; You refined us like silver…we went through fire and water, but You brought us to a place of abundance."

We had days when we felt that we were doing well while trusting God in every way. Then someone (even our missionary friends) would say, "Why don't you just give Hannah-Joy back to the orphanage and go home?" But we were bonded to Hannah-Joy and it was unthinkable for us to even consider doing that! God had led us to adopt Hannah-Joy and we wanted to honor Him in having her grow up knowing Christ. It was never an option for us to give her back to an institution. Every time we were notified of another setback in the adoption process, it forced us to our knees once again. We saw Hannah-Joy's adoption as a grave spiritual battle and only prayer wins those battles. Victor Hugo has said it better than I when he wrote, "There are times in a man's life when, regardless of the attitude of the body, the soul is on its knees in prayer."

Prayer became our modus operandi. It was the one refuge that brought us peace. But to stay in an attitude of peace took perpetual, conscious effort. God used prayer as the means of extricating us from our impossible situation. For months, we had tried EVERYTHING humanly possible to get the adoption of Hannah-Joy finalized. We had won our adoption case in the lower courts only to have the Solicitor General overturn our case and deny our legal right to her. And he was the highest law in the land. We had no other place to go EXCEPT to go over his head—to God. We had been told several times via the grapevine, "You will never get this child!" In utter desperation God continued to draw Les and me to Himself. HE was our only hope. We placed Hannah-Joy and ourselves before Him, asking for His mercy. The following verse became my daily reminder of that:

Psalm 33:10

*"The Lord nullifies the counsel of the nations;
He frustrates the plans of the people."*

There were times that I went before the Lord to remind Him of that particular verse in the Psalms. Then He would comfort my heart and mind with the knowledge that He is in charge, even over government officials.

Both Les and I came from very conservative spiritual and denominational backgrounds. But God began to chip away some of our preconceived ideas, traditions and teachings concerning how God works in a person's life. One morning when Hannah-Joy was two years old, I agonized in prayer over the whole adoption scenario. The Lord spoke very clearly and strongly to my heart, saying to me, "Call your Social Worker, Evelyn, and ask her about an 'inter- country adoption'." I was stunned by those words! Never could I recall hearing that term before that moment. But there was a sense of urgency that I felt in my heart from God! I went to the phone and called Les. I told him what the Lord had spoken to me. Les paused for a moment and then said, "You'd better call Evelyn now."

I dreaded that phone call to the DSWD. Previously, they had played games with me. They passed the phone from one person to another whenever I called to speak to Evelyn. It was frustrating and humiliating for me. But on that day when I called the DSWD, I talked with only one other person before they connected me with Evelyn. I posed my question to her using the words God had spoken to me—inter-country adoption. I asked her if there were such a thing as that.

"Why yes," she replied. "There are three ladies who handle these difficult adoptions." Then she gave me their names. I recognized the names of the first two ladies on the list. Les and I had prior experiences with both of them and they had not been good ones. But the third lady's name was unfamiliar to Les and me.

Before I called them, I prayed. I asked God, "Only allow me to speak to the right person." Then I dialed the phone. I called them in the same order Evelyn had given them to me. I thought that Evelyn might have had a purpose for how she placed them on the list. The first lady that I called was in a meeting and could not be disturbed. "Thank you, Father," I prayed. Lady number two was out of the office for the day. Once again I praised God that He had made those two ladies unavailable. It was 10 o'clock when I called the third lady. Her name was Divina Caalam (ka AH lam). Divina meant "divine." I was already encouraged just because of her name. I asked her if she worked with inter- country adoptions and, if so, could we meet with her to talk about it? Her answer was, "Yes, you can come at one o'clock today."

Quickly I called Vicki our attorney, who was also an attorney for the Pepsi Corporation. Then I called Les about our meeting with the DSWD. We asked Vicki to meet us at our house; then we could travel there together. Between the three of us, the decision was made to take Hannah-Joy with us. We wanted the DSWD to see her with us. We wanted them to see how bonded she was to us; we thought that it might make a difference in the decisions to be made. It was risky, though, as well. Because we had no legal right to her and due to the Solicitor General's actions against us, it was possible for us to lose her that very day.

Genesis 18:14

"Is anything too difficult for the Lord?"

We drove out to the DSWD across the city to their new office. I prayed silently and held Hannah-Joy in my lap while Les chatted with Vicki. After we arrived there and before going into the meeting, we sat in our car and prayed together once again. Our situation with Hannah-Joy was clearly in God's hands.

Mrs. Caalam's office was in the center of a very large room filled with many other desks. Initially we sensed an awkwardness or even aloofness on her part. We chatted for a few moments about things unrelated to our adoption. Les and I spoke some Tagalog, along with English. Combining those two languages creates another language that the Filipinos call "Taglish" (TAHG lish). Les and I had taken Tagalog in language school. We could see that Mrs. Caalam appreciated the fact that we had wanted to learn her language. If you lived in Manila, it wasn't REALLY necessary to learn the Tagalog language. Still, we wanted to try to have an understanding of their language. And our WBT/SIL organization wanted us to have a workable vocabulary in Tagalog, too. We felt strongly that if a person had chosen to live in a foreign country, if at all possible, he/she needed to know the language.

Five or six minutes into our meeting with Mrs. Caalam, after answering some of her questions, she made an astounding statement. She said to us, "We are having a pre- adoptive parent picnic in two weeks and if you are still here, we'd like you both to attend." I stared at Vicki, who looked at Les. The three of us could not believe what we had just heard! We were stunned! "If you are still here in two weeks?" What was she saying to us? For 19 months we had struggled, prayed and tried to resolve the adoption situation of Hannah-Joy, but without success! Was she saying that we could go to the States with Hannah-Joy and within two weeks? Divina began to explain, "If Holt Adoption Agency in Eugene, Oregon will accept all of your paperwork (home studies, your police clearance, physicals, etc.), you will be permitted to leave with Hannah-Joy and finish your adoption in Texas. We will fax ALL of your information to Holt today. We should hear from them within 24 hours."

We tried to absorb all of what we had just heard and all of the new information. I wanted to fall on my knees right there with praise to God! Words to "The Doxology" flooded my heart and mind. Vicki, Les and I tried to act like normal people *as we left Divina's* office with Hannah-Joy, but we giggled and floated out to our car. Our joy was too fragile to process or understand at that moment. But we felt giddy with hope in our hearts and, at long last, victory seemed something within our grasp.

Psalm 126:3

"The Lord has done great things for us; we are glad."

All of our information was faxed to Holt. Then we waited and continued to pray. We called some of our friends in the States and our Pastor Lou Schneider in Conroe, Texas. We shared with him our latest news. The church had prayed for us, as did many others. But after 24 hours, there was still no word from Mrs. Caalam. And still there was no word from Holt after 36 hours. We were trying very hard NOT to call Mrs. Caalam. But after 45 hours of waiting, I called her. She said, "Oh, just now I got word from Holt Adoption Agency, and they said, 'Yes!'" I don't remember the remainder of our conversation because both Les and I were crying. We called our Koinonia friends and our attorneys, Vicki and Caesar, to share the news. There was so much rejoicing about our release to leave the Philippines WITH Hannah-Joy. No longer captives, we were free to leave with our heads held high because God had made it all possible. We were humbled as we recognized God's grace and mercy in Hannah-Joy's adoption.

Corinthians 12: 9 (NIV)

"...My grace is sufficient for you, for my power is made perfect in weakness."

So many things needed to be accomplished before we could leave the Philippines with Hannah-Joy—a Philippine passport for her, a US visa, medical clearances, etc. We were even required by the American Embassy to view a movie on immigration. We complied with whatever they asked of us. From the time of our meeting with Divina Caalam, it was only 17 days until we deplaned in Dallas, Texas. Our son Randy, his family, and our friends Gordon and Leslie Christian, were waiting to see us and to meet Hannah- Joy. It was a precious moment in our lives and the culmination of many, many answers to thousands of prayers. At long last we were home in Texas and WITH Hannah-Joy. She was two years and three months old.

We finalized Hannah-Joy's adoption later that same year on August 17, 1990. And on my birthday that same year, October 16, Hannah-Joy became a United States citizen. She was almost three-years old.

The day Hannah-Joy became an American Citizen

Psalm 71:16 (NIV)

*"I will come and proclaim your mighty acts,
O sovereign Lord…"*

2 Corinthians 4:7 (NIV)

"But we have this treasure in jars of clay to show this all- surpassing power is from God and not from us."

THE EPILOGUE

Presently, I live in Lubbock, TX. Hannah-Joy and Phillip Wright were married in 2010. They live in Maryland and have a one-year-old baby girl, Ava Leslie. Our son, Randy has a ranch about two hours from Lubbock. I rarely get to see him or his family. Our beautiful daughter, Vicki Lynn, died in her sleep of a massive heart attack in 2017. She just went to sleep and woke up in heaven. The grief has lessened some but her absence in my life grows daily. Les, my precious, loving, wonderful husband and partner for 58.5 years, passed away on November 6, 2019. The grief for him and Vicki Lynn remains constant. I keep my eyes on the skies awaiting the Rapture of Jesus, where I can be reunited with all of my "beloveds. "And I want you to know that I'm working on: BOOK TWO of OUR GOD STILL SPEAKS.

Les, Ginger and Hannah-Joy

Stay tuned for BOOK TWO. I have remained in Lubbock, TX, with my Misty doggie, who is a "rescue." She is my constant companion and she makes sure that I'm okay. What a blessing she is for me. You'll hear all about this little doggie, in book TWO. One final note, I want to say again, God has been so good to me. His love never lessens for me and I can't help but praise Him; the real reason for Book Two. Book TWO of OUR GOD STILL SPEAKS will be out shortly. It is also little vignettes of things, people and situations that have taken place since Les' death. It continues to show how God answers my prayers and His faithfulness to me in my life without my "beloveds," Les and Vicki Lynn.

The Metzler Family
Randy, Hannah-Joy, Les, Vicki and Virginia

Psalm 27:13-14.

"I would have despaired unless I would have believed that I would see the goodness of the Lord in the land of the living. Wait for the Lord; be strong and let your heart take courage; yes, wait for the Lord."

www.ingramcontent.com/pod-product-compliance
Lightning Source LLC
LaVergne TN
LVHW041708070526
838199LV00045B/1250